Passing Through the Fire

JOSHUA LAWRENCE CHAMBERLAIN IN THE CIVIL WAR

Brian Swartz

EMERGING CIVIL WAR SERIES

Chris Mackowski, series editor
Chris Kolakowski, chief historian

The Emerging Civil War Series

offers compelling, easy-to-read overviews of some of the Civil War's most important battles and stories.

Recipient of the Army Historical Foundation's Lieutenant General Richard G. Trefry Award for contributions to the literature on the history of the U.S. Army

Also part of the Emerging Civil War Series:

Aftermath of Battle: The Burial of the Civil War Dead
by Meg Groeling

Dawn of Victory: Breakthrough at Petersburg, March 25 – April 2, 1865
by Edward Alexander

Don't Give an Inch: The Second Day at Gettysburg – from Little Round Top to Cemetery Ridge, July 2, 1863
by Chris Mackowski, Kristopher D. White, and Daniel T. Davis

Embattled Capital: A Guide to Richmond During the Civil War
by Robert M. Dunkerly and Doug Crenshaw

Grant's Left Hook: The Bermuda Hundred Campaign, May 5 – June 7, 1864
by Sean Michael Chick

Hellmira: The Union's Most Infamous Civil War Prison Camp – Elmira, NY
by Derek Maxfield

A Mortal Blow to the Confederacy: The Fall of New Orleans, 1862
by Mark F. Bielski

Simply Murder: The Battle of Fredericksburg, December 13, 1862
by Chris Mackowski and Kristopher D. White

To the Bitter End: Appomattox, Bennett Place, and the Surrenders of the Confederacy
by Robert M. Dunkerly

Unlike Anything that Ever Floated: The Monitor, Virginia, and the Battle of Hampton Roads, March 8 – 9, 1862
by Dwight Sturtevant Hughes

For a complete list of titles in the Emerging Civil War Series, visit www.emergingcivilwar.com.

Also by Brian Swartz:

Maine at War Volume I: Bladensburg to Sharpsburg (Epic Saga, 2019)

Passing Through the Fire

JOSHUA LAWRENCE CHAMBERLAIN IN THE CIVIL WAR

Brian Swartz

EMERGING CIVIL WAR SERIES

SB

Savas Beatie

California

First edition, first printing

ISBN-13 (paperback): 978-1-61121-561-8
ISBN-13 (ebook): 978-1-61121-562-5

Library of Congress Cataloging-in-Publication Data

Names: Swartz, Brian, 1954- author.
Title: Passing Through the Fire: Joshua Lawrence Chamberlain in the Civil War / by Brian Swartz.
Other titles: Joshua Lawrence Chamberlain in the Civil War
Description: El Dorado Hills, CA : Savas Beatie, [2021] | Includes bibliographical references and index. | Summary: "Drawing on Chamberlain's extensive memoirs and writings and multiple period sources, historian Brian F. Swartz follows Chamberlain across Maryland, Pennsylvania, and Virginia while examining the determined warrior who let nothing prevent him from helping save the United States"-- Provided by publisher.
Identifiers: LCCN 2020055333 | ISBN 9781611215618 (paperback) | ISBN 9781611215625 (ebook)
Subjects: LCSH: Chamberlain, Joshua Lawrence, 1828-1914. | United States--History--Civil War, 1861-1865--Campaigns. | Generals--United States--Biography. | United States--History--Civil War, 1861-1865--Regimental histories. | United States. Army. Corps, 5th (1862-1865) | Brewer (Me.)--Biography.
Classification: LCC E467.1.C47 .S93 2021 | DDC 355.0092 [B]--dc23
LC record available at https://lccn.loc.gov/2020055333

Published by
Savas Beatie LLC
989 Governor Drive, Suite 102
El Dorado Hills, California 95762
Phone: 916-941-6896
Email: sales@savasbeatie.com
Web: www.savasbeatie.com

Savas Beatie titles are available at special discounts for bulk purchases in the United States by corporations, institutions, and other organizations. For more details, please contact Special Sales, P.O. Box 4527, El Dorado Hills, CA 95762, or you may e-mail us at sales@savasbeatie.com, or visit our website at www.savasbeatie.com for additional information.

In memory of my beloved sister, Tracey Smith
(1958-2021)

Table of Contents

Footnotes for this volume are available at:
http://emergingcivilwar.com/publications/the-emerging-civil-war-series/footnotes

List of Maps

Maps by Edward Alexander

For the Emerging Civil War Series

Theodore P. Savas, *publisher*
Chris Mackowski, *series editor*
Christopher Kolakowski, *chief historian*
Sarah Keeney, *editorial consultant*
Kristopher D. White, *co-founding editor*

Publication supervision by Chris Mackowski
Design and layout by Savannah Rose

Acknowledgments

This wartime biography of Joshua L. Chamberlain would not be possible without the support and guidance of Chris Mackowski, who invited me to write about Chamberlain, with whom I share a hometown.

Thank you so much, Chris, for your confidence in me writing my first biography.

Many other people generously assisted me in finding historical material, both written and photographic, about the Chamberlain family. With deepest gratitude for their magnificent contributions to this book, I especially thank:

Steven Garrett, president of the Joshua L. Chamberlain Civil War Round Table and enthusiastic Pejepscot History Center member

Edward Alexander, mapmaker extraordinaire

Ashley Towle, Ph.D., lecturer in the Department of History and Honors, University of Southern Maine

Dedicated on November 11, 1954, and originally operated as a toll bridge, the Joshua Chamberlain Bridge spans the Penobscot River between Bangor, Maine, and Chamberlain's hometown of Brewer. (bfs)

Antietam was the first battlefield seen by Joshua L. Chamberlain and the 20th Maine. (bfs)

Ryan Quint, a historian with Emerging Civil War

Heather Moran, reference and outreach archivist at the Maine State Archives

Catherine Cyr, Pejepscot Historical Society museum services manager

Tom Desjardin, Civil War historian and author and 20th Maine Infantry and Joshua Chamberlain biographer

Roberta Schwarz, research services archivist in the George J. Mitchell Department of Special Collections & Archives, Bowdoin College Library

Desiree Butterfield-Nagy, reference archivist and librarian in the Special Collections Department, Raymond Fogler Library at the University of Maine

Matthew Bishop, Bangor (Maine) Historical Society curator

Darren French, library director of the Brewer Public Library

Betsy Paradis, local history and special collections librarian, and Elizabeth Stevens, local history assistant, Bangor Public Library

David Hanna, Brewer (Maine) Historical Society president

And last, but certainly not least, my dear wife, Susan, who has traipsed the Chamberlain battlefields with me.

PHOTO CREDITS:
Bangor Historical Society (bhs); Bangor Maine Public Library (bmpl); Brewer Maine Historical Society (bmhs); Brewer Public Library (bpl); Civil War Trust (cwt); Raymond Fogler Library, University of Maine (rfl); George J. Mitchell Dept. of Special Collections & Archives, Bowdoin College Library (bcl); Steven Garrett (sg); Harper's Weekly (hw); Library of Congress (loc); Chris Mackowski (cm); Maine State Archives (msa); National Archives (na); Onondaga Historical Association (oha); Pejepscot History Center Collection (phcc); Brian F. Swartz (bfs)

$\mathcal{F}$ oreword

BY THOMAS A. DESJARDIN

Back in 1990, a little-known documentary filmmaker from New Hampshire, inspired by an almost unknown novel about the battle of Gettysburg, aired his latest film about the Civil War and introduced a character from that novel to his viewers, most of whom had no idea the soldier had existed. The character was a Union army regimental commander who had trained as a minister, and the filmmaker gave credit for inspiring his own work to the depiction of this one soldier in a novel published 15 years earlier.

"But what was important to me about the book," he later said, "was that it introduced me, for the first time, to Joshua Lawrence Chamberlain. And for all intents and purposes, it was the life of Chamberlain which convinced me to embark on the most difficult and satisfying experience of my life." That filmmaker was Ken Burns, and that "satisfying experience" was the most watched program in the history of public television, the nine-episode series "The Civil War." The book which held the story of Chamberlain and grabbed Burns was Michael Shaara's The Killer Angels.

This now immortal triumvirate of Civil War memory—Burns, Shaara, and Chamberlain—has inspired a remarkable two-decade renaissance in Civil War scholarship. Perhaps Burns's greatest accomplishment was reigniting a passion in the hearts and minds of tens of millions of American viewers for the history of our nation's bloodiest war.

A simplified version of the 20th Maine monument in Gettysburg stands atop a rocky outcropping in Chamberlain Freedom Park in Brewer, Maine. (cm)

The 20th Maine marker at Gettysburg was dedicated by veterans of the regiment on October 3, 1889. Speaking at the ceremony, Chamberlain praised his fellows: "every one here, officer and soldier, did more than his duty, and acted with utmost intelligence and spirit. . . ." (cm)

Across the nation, descendants of Civil War veterans went up to the attics of the old family homes and opened the trunks that contained the papers, letters, uniforms, and equipment that might have otherwise been lost to time. From these attics and local historical collections, these long unseen gems of historical knowledge went to safer, more accessible repositories where scholars, researchers, and writers could glean new information to pass on to the rest of us.

One great thing about history is that over time, researchers discover new and enlightening things about a given subject that change what we thought we knew about it. This reality has never been more evident since new technologies helped make previously unexplored archival collections available to everyone with an Internet connection.

Every day, workers at historical repositories digitize more information and place it in searchable databases that researchers worldwide can easily access. More primary-source material becomes available to scholars and hobbyists alike who have more information on which to base their research and thus our understanding of their subjects.

The explosion of interest in the Civil War that Michael Shaara and Joshua Chamberlain helped Ken Burns to ignite in 1990 broadened through the years that followed when Jeff Daniels brought Chamberlain to life on the big screen—twice—in feature films that gained cult followings on home-video platforms.

Coming neatly full circle, the story of Chamberlain that helped shake loose generations of valuable historical information has also helped us to learn more about the man himself, adding to and peeling back the layers of a complicated person and his life story.

It is in all of this context that makes the new work by Brian Swartz so valuable. It has been a good many years since the publication of a study of the period of Chamberlain's life from the day he agreed to join the Union army to the day he was mustered out nearly three years later. It is not just the number of years, either, that make them valuable, but also their quality in terms of the newly discovered information made accessible for the first time that enables a much more rich and robust depiction and understanding of Chamberlain's military experience.

With his characteristic eye for good research material and a knack for finding the most obscure, yet enlightening letter, report, or memoir, Brian Swartz has brought together the latest and most voluminous collection of Chamberlain's life in wartime and ably brought it to us to enjoy and to learn from.

Those who are embarking on their first real expedition with the Maine minister-turned-warrior— our own Killer Angel—will find much to enjoy in the pages that follow. Likewise, the wily old Chamberlain aficionado will also benefit from the fruits of Swartz's labors, making use of the new material that has come into the public realm since anyone closely examined Chamberlain in the Civil War.

Maine native THOMAS A. DESJARDIN *has authored, among other books,* Stand Firm Ye Boys From Maine: The 20th Maine and the Gettysburg Campaign; Joshua L. Chamberlain: A Life in Letters; *and* These Honored Dead: How the Story of Gettysburg Shaped American Memory. *He worked as a National Park Service archivist and historian at Gettysburg National Military Park and served as the historical advisor to actor Jeff Daniels during the filming of* Gettysburg.

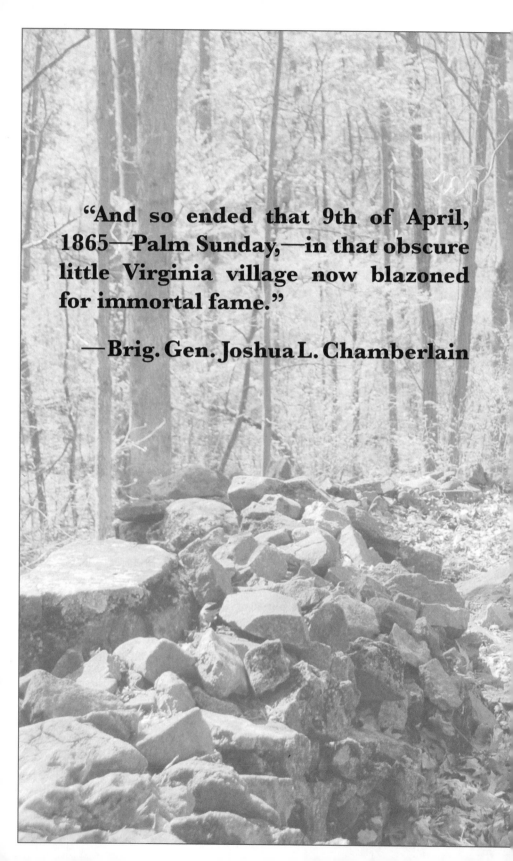

"And so ended that 9th of April, 1865—Palm Sunday,—in that obscure little Virginia village now blazoned for immortal fame."

—Brig. Gen. Joshua L. Chamberlain

Prologue

As the Maryland hardwoods shifted to autumnal glory, Lt. Col. Joshua L. Chamberlain steered his horse up a South Mountain slope on this fine fall 1862 day, either Friday, October 24 or Saturday, October 25. Assigned as "officer of the day" for the 3rd Brigade, 1st Division, V Corps, he checked the advance picket posts beyond the divisional camps near Sharpsburg in Washington County. Second-in-command of the 20th Maine, Chamberlain savored these official outings. He often rode "into some rich shaded valley, craggy defile, or along some lovely stream," the waterways flowing south toward the nearby Potomac River.

On this particular day, he rode atop "one of these blue hills, where the view stretches forty miles into Virginia." From the saddle, Chamberlain gazed at distant "villages & streams & bright patches of cultivated fields." He especially noticed the military threat: Robert E. Lee's Army of Northern Virginia, or at least the large contingent camped "fifteen or twenty miles away." Over there beyond the Potomac glowed "the long lines of rebel fires."

Over there, Confederates cooked their meals and sat near the flames to keep warm in the damp, cool weather. The 20th Maine lads loitered similarly around their campfires near Antietam Ford; rain and chill spared no soldier, no matter how righteous his political leaders considered their own cause.

Turning his head westward in the clear air, Chamberlain gazed at Sharpsburg "on our own

The bronze Chamberlain statue in Brewer, Maine, was sculpted by Glenn and Dianne Hines and dedicated in 1996. (bfs)

side" of the Potomac. He saw "the great battle field of Antietam—the hills trodden bare & the fields all veined with the tracks of artillery trains, or movements of Army corps."

There, the 20th Maine had guarded the Middle Bridge over Antietam Creek as Confederates and Yankees slaughtered each other on Wednesday, September 17. Their viewpoint "broken by clumps of trees and distant hill-tops," the Mainers had watched Maj. Gen. Joseph Hooker and I Corps advance, noted Pvt. Theodore Gerrish, Co. H. The distant "hillsides flamed with fire. There was a fearful roar, and all were concealed by clouds of smoke," said Gerrish, awed by the first combat violence witnessed by him, Chamberlain, and their regimental comrades.

Unionists rapturously welcomed George McClellan as he entered Frederick, Maryland. (hw)

The fighting had raged through the afternoon. Downstream on the Union left, "those terrible volleys of musketry, the ceaseless din of artillery, the clouds of smoky dust" moved "toward Sharpsburg" as Maj. Gen. Ambrose Burnside and IX Corps pushed across Antietam Creek, Gerrish noticed. He saw the courier hurling a foam-covered horse across the Middle Bridge and "up the dusty highway" to find

The 20th Maine guarded the Middle Bridge over Antietam Creek. (loc)

Maj. Gen. George McClellan. Send help! Burnside implored as Ambrose Powell Hill and his hard-marching Confederates arrived from Harper's Ferry. But "too timid and slow for a great commander," McClellan hesitated, and Powell, in a quaint Maine expression, "stove in" the Union left and stabilized Lee's right. Antietam cost McClellan 12,410 casualties, Lee 10,316 men, including a thousand or so missing.

The next day Chamberlain rode across the Lower Bridge, now immortalized as "Burnside's Bridge," as the 20th Maine moved nearer Sharpsburg, still occupied by Confederates. However, the soldiers in gray vanished overnight, and on Friday, the Maine lads had marched to Sharpsburg across terrain splattered with dead and stinking men and horses. Shedding their first blood at Saturday's Shepherdstown Ford fight, the 20th Mainers wound up camping at the Antietam Iron Works near Antietam Creek.

Now, a little over a month later, on this perch downriver from Sharpsburg, Chamberlain—clad in "my one suit of clothing" now "a little worn & a little thin"—could have turned his eyes from the Antietam battlefield and looked again into Virginia.

Over there, the Confederates awaited him. Given the chance, they would kill him.

They certainly would try.

George McClellan established his headquarters at Pry House during Antietam. (bfs)

Joshua Chamberlain and the 20th Maine crossed Burnside Bridge on September 18, 1862. (bfs)

The Professor Goes to War

CHAPTER ONE

JULY 14 - SEPTEMBER 7, 1862

Artillery thundering behind him, 34-year-old Lt. Col. Joshua L. Chamberlain witnessed a Virginia city dying around mid-day on Thursday, December 11, 1863. He and Adjutant John M. Brown of the 20th Maine sat their horses near the Rappahannock River's east bank, opposite Fredericksburg. Mississippi infantrymen occupied its built-up section, and other Confederate troops held both Marye's Heights behind the town and the hills stretching southwest from the city. Hidden in shattered buildings, the Mississippians shot Union engineers assembling a pontoon bridge toward the Fredericksburg shore. To dislodge the snipers, Union Maj. Gen. Ambrose Burnside hurled a 150-cannon tirade from Stafford Heights, rising behind the 20th Maine officers.

Colonel Adelbert Ames, commander of the 20th Maine, had granted them permission earlier to ride to the Lacey House (Chatham Manor), where they made "with some of the rashness of youth. . . quite a minute inspection of things," Chamberlain said.

He saw in Fredericksburg "lurid bursts, where some enormous shell had lifted a brick building in the air, ground to dust." The lovely colonial town was "on fire in a dozen places, columns of smoke streaming into the sky" amidst "the thunder and scream of artillery," The view "was grand beyond anything I ever witnessed, or expected to witness," remembered Chamberlain, so close to the city that he could see

Beyond the Joshua L. Chamberlain statue in Brunswick, Maine, stands the First Parish Church where Chamberlain married Frances "Fanny" Adams on December 7, 1855. (bfs)

Joshua L. Chamberlain
initially considered the
ministry as a career. (bcl)

"the rebel sharpshooters running from the shells, and rallying to the front again."

Did he notice the similar topography between Fredericksburg and his hometown of Brewer, Maine? As the Rappahannock does at Fredericksburg, the Penobscot River separates Brewer on the east bank from larger Bangor—that "beautiful and busy city," Chamberlain called it—on the west bank. And as at Fredericksburg, the terrain rises away from the Bangor and Brewer shorelines. Bangor, a "picturesque cluster of buildings," climbs quickly over higher ground split by the Kenduskeag Stream ravine. Like Fredericksburg, streets ran uphill in Bangor, and the cross-river views were unobstructed in late 1862. In Brewer, the "monumental headland" near where Chamberlain grew up drops off downriver to flatter terrain backed by a long ridge.

On this December Thursday, did he imagine artillery deployed in Brewer pounding apart Bangor?

*   *   *

He had come far since leaving Brewer, where he was born Lawrence Joshua Chamberlain to Joshua and Sarah Dupee (Brastow) Chamberlain on September 8, 1828. Siblings Horace Beriah, Sarah "Sae" Brastow, John Calhoun, and Thomas Davee followed through 1841. Always called "Lawrence" by his relatives, the eldest Chamberlain sibling switched his first and middle names after moving to Brunswick.

Growing up on his parents' 100-acre farm on Chamberlain Street in Brewer, Chamberlain became physically strong from working the land and chopping firewood. Both reading and music appealed to him, as

Chamberlain was born on
September 8, 1828, in this
house in Brewer. (bmhs)

did sailing, learned during family jaunts on Penobscot Bay aboard the schooner *Lapwing*. His family attended Brewer's First Congregational Church, and Chamberlain developed his Christian faith there.

Sent at age 14 to a military academy operated by Lt. Charles Jarvis Whiting at "The Crags" on the Bangor Road in North Ellsworth, he gained "some practical acquaintance with the French language." Chamberlain taught himself Greek, a requisite language for incoming freshmen at Bowdoin College in Brunswick. After graduating in 1852, he spent three years studying theology at Bangor Theological Seminary "and received a license to preach," but the ministry held little appeal. Bowdoin hired him as an instructor in mid-decade, and he left Brewer permanently for Brunswick.

Joshua L. Chamberlain was close to his mother, Sarah Dupee Brastow Chamberlain. (bpl)

By then he was engaged to Frances "Fanny" Caroline Adams, sent at age four by her birth parents, Ashur and Amelia Wyllys Adams of Jamaica Plain in Massachusetts, to live in Brunswick with Ashur's nephew, Reverend George Adams, and his wife, Sarah Ann. George was the long-time minister at Brunswick's First Parish Church; he and Sarah—and after her death, his next wife, Helen—offered Fanny a middle-class upbringing that her own parents could not.

With Reverend Adams presiding, Joshua and Fanny married on December 7, 1855 and spent their wedding night in the Adams' house. Bowdoin named the new husband a "full professor of rhetoric and oratory" in 1856; daughter Grace Dupee ("Daisy") arrived that year on October 16.

A second child, "a son, three months premature," born on November 19, 1857, "lived but a few hours," and went to his grave nameless. Born in October 1858, Harold Wyllys survived to adulthood, as did Grace. Born in May 1860, daughter Emily Stelle died that September.

Horace Chamberlain died from tuberculosis in December 1861, not long after Joshua and Daisy visited him in Brewer. Always close to his siblings, for Joshua the mourning became nonstop.

Joshua Chamberlain was the father of Joshua L. Chamberlain. (bpl)

The Civil War's beginning in April 1861 had prompted the calls for volunteer soldiers. During the mid-1862 summons for 300,000 men, the Lincoln administration required Maine to raise four infantry

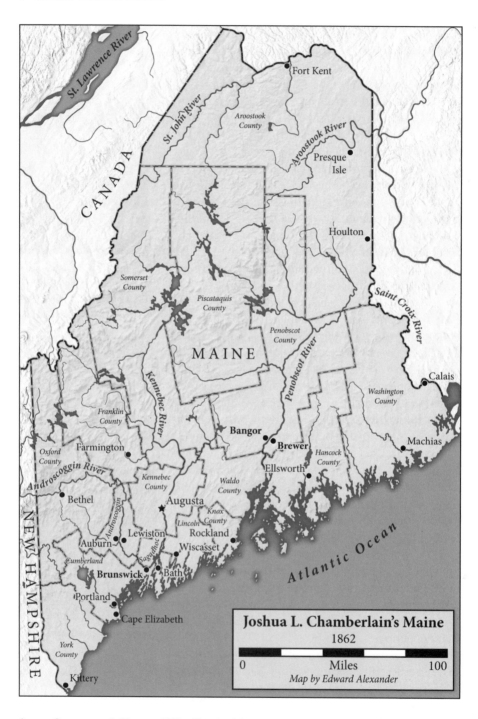

JOSHUA CHAMBERLAIN'S MAINE IN 1862—Chamberlain grew up in a decidedly rural Maine that, with a population hovering around 630,000 people, would send approximately 73,000 men into the army during the Civil War.

regiments. Authorized by Governor Israel Washburn Jr., "private individuals . . . at their own expense" recruited men and expected commissions "as a reward" to be granted "in the companies which they might raise," said Wiscasset schoolmaster Ellis Spear, a Bowdoin College graduate ('58) and aspiring soldier. Wanting to command "a military company . . . when he scarcely knew a line of battle from a line of rail fence," Spear scoured Lincoln, Knox, Sagadahoc, and Waldo counties for 100 recruits.

Joshua Chamberlain worshiped at Brewer's First Congregational Church. (bmhs)

Meanwhile, 33-year-old professor Joshua Chamberlain wrote Washburn from Brunswick on Monday, July 14, "In pursuance of the offer of reinforcements for the war, I ask if your Excellency desires and will accept my service." Chamberlain had planned to leave Bowdoin "to spend a year or more in Europe, in the service of the College," but duty called. "This war, so costly in blood and treasure, will not cease" until Northerners "are willing to leave good positions, and sacrifice the dearest personal interests, to rescue our Country from Desolation. . . . Every man ought to come forward and ask to be placed at his proper post," wrote Chamberlain. "Yours to command."

Receiving the letter on Tuesday, Washburn responded favorably, asking Chamberlain to meet him at the Maine State House on July 18. Already "several young [Bowdoin] graduates" wanted "to go with me as privates or in any way," he wrote the governor on July 17. "I know my men, & know whom to pick."

His initial letters to Washburn revealed an innate confidence and self-knowledge. "I know how to learn"

Joshua Chamberlain lived in Maine Hall during his last three years at Bowdoin College. (sg)

After graduating from Bowdoin College, Chamberlain studied for the ministry at the Bangor Theological Seminary. (bhs)

what Chamberlain did not already know pertaining to "military matters," and he could "get together a thousand men in a very short time." Critics might call him cocky, but "I believe you will find me qualified," he told Washburn.

Chamberlain was "a graceful, erect gentleman of medium but strong build, with a finely shaped head, a classic forehead and nose, a moustache that swept back with a distinguished flair, a resonant and pleasing voice," biographer John Pullen described the professor.

The news about the governor's favorable reaction to Chamberlain spurred recommendations fair and foul. Brunswick physician John Dunlap Lincoln (Bowdoin '43) wrote Washburn on July 17 that "we are all here very much gratified" about the news. Chamberlain "is a gentleman and scholar" and "a man both of energy and sense and in our opinion as capable of commanding a Reg't as any . . . West Point graduate." Writing Washburn about Chamberlain from Portland, Maine Attorney General Josiah H. Drummond huffed that "his old classmates etc. here say that you have been deceived: that C. is nothing at all: that is the universal expression of those who knew him."

Frances "Fanny" Caroline Adams married Joshua L. Chamberlain in December 1855. (bcl)

Chamberlain's plans upset the Bowdoin balance of power. The faculty vied with the administration and the trustees "for the control of the College," and as professor of modern languages, Chamberlain "held . . . a strategic position" tilting power toward the faculty. If he left, most qualified candidates "were . . . not of the [same] strict orthodox persuasion" as he, and the faculty feared his replacement "would be . . . one of the adverse party," thus tilting power the other direction. So, the Bowdoin faculty told Washburn that Chamberlain "had no military stuff in him" and "that he was . . . only a mild-mannered commonplace student." The professor, who

had not shared his career change with "his colleagues"
sloughed off their "injurious misrepresentations," and
Washburn, who "well knew"
the professor's father and
grandfather, ignored the
faculty altogether.

Rumors flew. "The
son of Colonel Joshua
Chamberlain of Brewer . .
. accepted the Colonelcy of
the Maine 20th Regiment,"
Bangor newspaper publisher
William Wheelden reported
on July 22. "This is a significant and gratifying index
to the State of public feeling in the present crisis."

The "bird-colonel" rumor possibly started when
Chamberlain, while keeping "a discrete silence" to
everyone else as to why he visited Augusta, let slip
"in a private conversation" with Brig. Gen. Oliver
Otis Howard in Brunswick that Washburn "thought
favorably of my having it," command of "a new
Regt." Chamberlain asserted to Washburn that "these
mortifying reports . . . did not come from me in any way
that I can imagine. These reports and contradictions . . .
are so embarrassing to me."

So many men enlisted in regiments 16 to 19 that
when Secretary of War Edwin M. Stanton asked for
another regiment in early August, Maine Adjutant
General John L. Hodsdon ordered that "all companies
already enlisted for new regiments," but not needed,
must report by August 12 at Island Park in Portland.
These disparate companies became "the Twentieth of
Maine Volunteers."

Joshua and Fanny
Chamberlain spent their
wedding night in her father's
house, the First Parish Church
parsonage in Brunswick. (sg)

LEFT— Governor Israel
Washburn Jr. swiftly
transitioned Maine to a
wartime footing. (msa)

RIGHT— Maine Adjutant
General John Hodsdon
capably administered the
state's war effort. (bmpl)

Horace Beriah Chamberlain, second oldest of the five Chamberlain siblings, was a Bowdoin College graduate. (bcl)

An 1861 West Point graduate from Rockland in Knox County, Adelbert Ames suffered a bad leg wound while fighting with the 5th U.S. Artillery at First Manassas. Promoted to brevet lieutenant colonel as the Peninsula Campaign ended, he traveled to Maine and lobbied for a colonelcy in a new infantry regiment. Giving Ames the 20th Maine, Washburn made Chamberlain its lieutenant colonel and Capt. Charles D. Gilmore (a 7th Maine veteran) of Bangor its major. All three were commissioned on August 8.

Irritated at the "unexpected degree of opposition" from the Bowdoin faculty," which had urged Washburn "to withhold my commission," Chamberlain wrote in separate August 8 letters to the governor that "I shall accept" the commission and "present the matter to the Faculty . . . & an hour will settle it."

Still in Brunswick on August 15, Chamberlain recommended four names for 20th Maine positions. Having clerked in a Bangor store, brother Tom Chamberlain sought quartermaster sergeant, "and I should like to have him receive the appointment."

When Chamberlain left Brunswick as a lieutenant colonel, "the faculty offered no congratulations." Brunswick and Topsham residents, however, gave him "the most splendid and famous horse in the region, with a full set of elegant equipments." He reported to the 20th Maine's camp on Monday, August 18. "By hook or crook the ten companies were raised" and sent to Camp Mason in Cape Elizabeth, Ellis Spear said.

Joshua L. Chamberlain possibly visited the Maine State House for the first time when summoned there by the governor in July 1862. (msa)

Lacking clothing and most military items, the recruits made do, as Mainers are wont, with what was available. Captains organized their companies. Gilmore "organized a guard," with "his first officer of the day" turned out "in a brown cutaway, striped trowsers, and a silk hat" and carrying a ramrod because he lacked a sword, Spear chuckled.

Adelbert Ames reached Camp Mason one late August evening and went to "the Headquarters' tent."

LEFT— Maine Attorney General Josiah Drummond disparaged Joshua L. Chamberlain. (msa))

RIGHT— Maine native Oliver Otis Howard lost his right arm at Seven Pines. (loc)

The "half loafing" guard "did not salute" before commenting, "'How do you do, Colonel'?

"It was his first experience with volunteers," Spear said of Ames, "and he found them in their most immature condition." Sending for the officer of the day (possibly Spear), Ames fired off questions that the captain, "as ignorant as a spring chicken," could not answer. "A hell of a regiment," muttered Ames.

Ironically, the acerbic Ames developed a close relationship with Chamberlain and taught him the fine points of army regulations, regimental organization, and an officer's duties. Chamberlain read the field manual *Casey's Tactics* at night, asked Ames questions, and continued learning as the regiment coalesced.

The 20th Maine mustered on Friday, August 29. Ellis Spear got his captaincy, and his 100 recruits became Co. G. On Tuesday, September 2, the "regiment of uniformed, but unarmed men marched from Camp Mason, near Portland . . . to the railroad depot" to catch the Boston train, recalled Pvt. Theodore Gerrish, Co. H. Two locomotives hauling 21 railroad cars left the depot at 6:20 a.m.

Wounded at Bull Run, Mainer Adelbert Ames sought a regimental colonelcy in summer 1862. (loc)

Unloading at North Station, the 20th Maine tramped through the Beantown streets to a wharf and packed aboard the steamship *Merrimac* along with the 36th Massachusetts. The ship docked at Alexandria, Virginia, on Saturday, September 6. The 20th Maine lads marched seven miles upriver, camped, and boarded "a small steamer for Washington" on Sunday, said Gerrish. Put ashore, the Maine boys marched to the federal arsenal. That night Joshua Chamberlain slept "in an . . . open lot" adjacent to the arsenal, "on a downy bed of dead cats, bricks and broken bottles," recalled Spear.

Horror on the Heights

CHAPTER TWO

SEPTEMBER 8 - DECEMBER 16, 1862

Joshua Chamberlain spent his 34th birthday getting a proper introduction to army life. On Monday, September 8, the men of the 20th Maine drew Enfield rifles, 40 rounds of ammunition apiece, and other equipment at the Washington, D.C., arsenal, then marched that "hot September evening . . . without a halt, seven miles" to Fort Craig in Arlington, Virginia, recalled Capt. Ellis Spear.

"It was a most ludicrous march," with "an untrained drum corps" rattling the ill-stepping regiment past incredulous civilians and across the Long Bridge, said Pvt. Theodore Gerrish, Co. H. The 20th Maine men "marched, ran, walked, galloped" to reach Fort Craig. Laden with rifled muskets and full military gear, the men grumbled loudly during that "moonlight march of four or five miles," recalled Pvt. Samuel L. Miller, Co. F. The regiment's commander, Col. Adelbert Ames, endured the noisy, accordion-like marching a while, then exploded. "If you can't do any better than you have tonight, you better all desert and go home!" he shouted.

At Fort Craig, the 20th Maine joined the "Light Brigade" (3rd Brigade), formerly commanded by Brig. Gen. Daniel Butterfield. Bloodied while holding the Union's extreme left flank at Gaines' Mill and now led by Col. Thomas Baylis Whitmore Stockton, the brigade included Brady's Company of Massachusetts Sharpshooters; the 16th Michigan; the 12th, 17th, and 44th New York; and the 83rd Pennsylvania.

In Fredericksburg, a view from Marye's Heights looks down on the infamous stone wall and sunken road, as well as the Martha Innis house. Federals attacked across an open plain beyond the wall. (cm)

A native New Yorker and a West Point graduate ('27), Stockton served in the Mexican-American War and moved to Michigan in the late 1850s. The 16th Michigan's first colonel, he got the 3rd Brigade in September 1861. Captured at Gaines' Mill, he had rejoined the brigade after his Libby Prison confinement. Stockton reported to Maj. Gen. George W. Morell, commanding the 1st Division, V Corps (Maj. Gen. Fitz John Porter). Colonel James Barnes had the 1st Brigade, Brig. Gen. Charles Griffin the 2nd Brigade.

Pursuing Robert E. Lee, the 1st Division lurched into Maryland on Friday, September 12, passed through Frederick two days later to camp at Middletown, and crossed South Mountain via Turner's Gap to camp Tuesday, September 16, near the Middle Bridge across Antietam Creek at Sharpsburg. Major General George B. McClellan held V Corps in reserve on September 17 during the bloody battle.

Joshua Chamberlain relished the natural beauty of South Mountain and rural Maryland. (bfs)

Lee withdrew across the Potomac River to Shepherdstown, Virginia, via Boeteler's (Blackburn's) Ford on September 19. McClellan told Porter to support Union cavalry pursuing the Confederate rear guard, now atop the bluffs overlooking the ford and a mill dam about a half mile upriver. By sunset, Porter had pushed some troops across the Potomac but withdrew them a few hours later.

McClellan ordered a stronger V Corps probe, so Brig. Gen. George Sykes's men (2nd Division) crossed the river about 7:00 a.m. on September 20 with the 2nd Brigade of Maj. Charles Lovell. "The enemy, about 3000 strong, with artillery" soon appeared, and Sykes pulled Lovell's regulars back to the bluffs. Jim Barnes started his seven-regiment 1st Brigade across Boeteler's Ford around 9:00 a.m. Forming on the bluffs just west of Lovell, the brigade traded fire with enemy skirmishers. Colonel Gouverneur K. Warren brought his 2nd Brigade (two New York regiments) up on Lovell's left flank.

While Union artillery posted above the Chesapeake & Ohio Canal fired on the advancing

Union troops fire at Confederate infantry on the Shepherdstown, Virginia bluffs. (loc)

enemy, Thomas Stockton started his brigade through Boeteler's Ford. "The river was wide, the water deep, the current swift," said Theodore Gerrish, busy feeling his way across narrow ledges to the Virginia shore. He remembered the 20th Maine climbing the bluffs, forming, and shooting at Confederates. Those 3rd Brigade components that crossed the river "pushed out a short distance," recalled Pvt. Samuel Miller, Co. F.

Orders recalled the Maine boys. Riding "a magnificent horse," Ames (as Gerrish's identification alluded) "sat coolly" in the river near the south bank, "speaking pleasantly to the men as they passed him."

Sometime before the 20th Maine waded into Virginia, Maj. Charles Gilmore lent Lt. Col. Joshua L. Chamberlain a "black horse . . . to avoid exposing my splendid white horse 'Prince' to enemy fire." During the retreat, Chamberlain steered his mount into the river's middle to warn retreating soldiers about a particularly deep hole. Enemy bullets missed him, but "his horse, however, was not so lucky." A bullet hit the animal "in [the] head near bit of bridle," so "Chamberlain joined the foot soldiers wading to safety."

Boteler's Ford spans the Potomac River between Sharpsburg, Maryland and Shepherdstown, West Virginia. (loc)

Private Hezekiah Long of Co. F recalled that a Union battery "got into position and gave the Rebels an unmerciful shelling, which was the only thing that saved us from being all cut up to pieces." Lying down

Joshua Chamberlain and his borrowed horse briefly served as a Potomac River navigation marker during the battle of Shepherdstown. (msa)

Rising from the Potomac River between Shepherdstown, Virginia (foreground), and Sharpsburg, Maryland, the piers of a destroyed railroad bridge are located about a half mile upstream from Boteler's Ford. (bfs)

on the bank separating the tow path from the dry C & O Canal, the Maine boys fired "a few shots at them across the River."

Union casualties totaled 363 men, including three soldiers wounded in the 20th Maine. Chamberlain had demonstrated a coolness under fire; he proudly informed Fanny that "we were ordered in to the fight & went. Then the Regt 'fired' abundantly at the crossing."

For the next three weeks, the 20th Maine helped guard the Maryland shore opposite Shepherdstown. The regiment shifted on October 7 near the Antietam Creek outlet, and marched for Harpers Ferry on October 30. Ames used the six weeks to give "the regiment a taste of discipline and drill which it so much needed," Miller said.

Men drilled by company and battalion, officers studied *Casey's Tactics,* and the "soldierly bearing of the regiment soon became conspicuous," Miller said. Chamberlain often spent "12 to 15 hours a day in the saddle" while serving as the brigade's officer of the day "every third day," responsible for "all the outposts & advanced guards," he wrote Fanny.

"Terrible sickness" afflicted the Maine lads, lacking shelter tents and for some weeks even great coats, Gerrish noted. Unsanitary conditions spread sickness, the autumn turned preternaturally cold and windy, and "strong men grew weak with disease" and died.

Yet Chamberlain, physically active during his youth, thrived while homesickness and depression stalked some 20th Mainers. Realizing how academia

had stifled his spirit, he would rather "spend my whole life in campaigning" than dealing with Bowdoin's collegiate intrigues, he told Fanny. "No danger & no hardship ever makes me wish to get back to that college life again," Chamberlain stated. "I can't breathe when I think of those last two years." Chamberlain had evidently chafed at paying obeisance to certain Bowdoin officials. Army life "& the habit of command will make me less complaisant—will break upon the notion that certain persons are the natural authorities over me," he wrote.

When Confederate cavalry withdrew to Virginia after raiding Chambersburg, Pennsylvania, the 20th Maine participated in the fruitless Union pursuit. (hw)

Fanny requested a daguerreotype of her husband and permission to visit him. "Does your innocent little head imagine that I could get a photograph (!) taken here?" Chamberlain chuckled. "My stars!" As for visiting the regimental camp, Fanny identified two colonels' wives "coming this way" from Maine, but the colonels were "stationed in permanent fortifications, or camps . . . quite in the rear as I understand," her husband explained.

He could not offer Fanny adequate quarters because "my rubber blanket is not quite big enough to accommodate ever so sweet & welcome a guest on the rough hill sides, or in the drenching valleys that constitute my changing homes." Yet had Fanny insisted on visiting, "I do not imagine any body would be more glad to see any body . . . who is the constant center of his every dream & the soul of his every thought!" Chamberlain confessed his love—and perhaps his lust— for his wife.

* * *

Having dawdled for six weeks after the Battle of Antietam, McClellan, prodded by Lincoln, finally pursued Lee. The 20th Maine crossed the Potomac and Shenandoah rivers on October 31 and marched through the Loudon Valley. Turning southeast, the Army of the Potomac reached the Warrenton area on November 9, and V Corps camped there a week.

Chamberlain attended the November 10 farewell reception held at corps' headquarters for McClellan, who had been sacked by Lincoln and replaced by Maj. Gen. Ambrose Burnside. Fifteen days later, the War Department had Fitz John Porter arrested on charges relating to Second Manassas; V Corps' revolving-door command went to Maj. Gen. Joseph Hooker, and Porter suffered a January 1863 court-martial and almost drum-head dismissal.

Planning to attack Lee by crossing the Rappahannock River above Fredericksburg and catching the Army of Northern Virginia on open ground, Burnside quickly marched his army rather than linger at Warrenton. The V Corps moved out in mid-month and camped along the Richmond, Fredericksburg, & Potomac Railroad in Stafford County. On November 24, the 20th Maine settled on "a small pine knoll at 'Stoneman's Switch,' near Falmouth," said Theodore Gerrish. Companies laid out their respective streets; similar camps spread for miles across the countryside.

President Abraham Lincoln met with George McClellan in early October 1862. (loc)

The RF&P Railroad reached the Potomac River at Aquia Landing, a muddy backwater. Army engineers built new wharves there and repaired the tracks to Stoneman's Switch, now a transfer point for the supplies shipped from Northern ports.

Unfortunately for Burnside, the pontoon boats needed for bridging the Rappahannock arrived so late that Confederates fortified the Fredericksburg heights before Union troops could cross the river. The jig was up, Burnside turned obstinate, and the Army of the Potomac fought. Hooker got the Center Grand Division, which included III and V corps. Dan Butterfield got the latter corps.

Leaving its camp at 5:30 a.m., Thursday, December 11, the 20th Maine marched some three miles south toward the Lacey House on Stafford Heights. The thudding artillery grew louder as Union gunners shelled Fredericksburg, and Chamberlain and Adjutant John M. Brown rode to watch the shelling.

On Friday, "we moved still nearer the river, but did not cross and, much to our disappointment, spent another night on the north side of the Rappahannock," groused a 20th Maine soldier using the pseudonym "W."

The weak sun gradually burned away the fog on Saturday, December 13. "During the forenoon we waited, listening to the almost uninterrupted roar of artillery and incessant volleys of musketry" rising from the plain south of Fredericksburg, wrote W. While other Union troops attacked Confederates defending Howison and Prospect Hills to the south, II and IX corps of the Right Grand Division would assault Marye's Heights. Enemy artillery perched atop it; Southern infantry spread along the stone wall bordering the summit-skirting Telegraph Road.

Wounded during an 1849 skirmish with Apaches, Ambrose Burnside left the army and invented his namesake carbine. (loc)

A 12-pounder Napoleon stands on Prospect Hill at Fredericksburg. (bfs)

Virginia planter William Fitzhugh constructed Chatham Manor in 1768-1771. (bfs)

Standing amidst the 1st Division near the Lacey House, the 20th Maine watched the disaster unfolding across the river. Involving the 3rd Division, II Corps, the first attack against the heights started about 11:00 a.m. Union brigades emerged from the city's ruins and formed, the "lines first steadily moving forward in perfect order and array, the flag high poised and leading," Chamberlain observed. A mill race with broken bridges disrupted the advance, and slight rises briefly hid Yankees here and there from Confederate view.

Enemy artillery fired, "the first range of shot and shell" leaving the lines "checked and broken," he noticed. "But bright bayonets fixed," the Union boys tramped onward until "reaching the last slope" beneath the stone wall, "suddenly illuminated by a sheet of flame."

Confederate infantrymen fired en masse, reached for rifles loaded by comrades, and fired steadily. Chamberlain saw "the whole [Union] line sinking as if swallowed up in earth," the regimental flags dropping, "and only a writhing mass marking that high-tide halt of uttermost manhood and supreme endeavor." Dragging wounded comrades, survivors pulled back below the last sheltering rise.

"There we stood for an hour, witnessing five immortal charges," Chamberlain soon noted. Maine men cried while watching the "thickening ridges of the fallen."

An order finally set V Corps in motion.
With Col. James Barnes and his 1st Brigade
leading, Charles Griffin's 1st Division crossed the
river on a Middle Crossing pontoon bridge. "The
rebels could see us perfectly well, and had the range
of the bridge and roads through which we had to
pass," and enemy shells whizzed past the 20th Maine,
Chamberlain said. "The crowding, swerving column
set the pontoons swaying, so that the horses reeled and
men could scarcely keep their balance," he realized.

Crossing the railroad tracks, the 3rd Brigade
formed, partially sheltered by "slightly rising ground"
already covered with Union
casualties. To the left, the
division's other brigades went
forward. With Ames walking
in front of the colors, the 20th
Maine "advanced in the face
of the most terrific cross fire
of artillery and musketry," said
Chamberlain, sent by Ames to
watch the right flank.

Moving uphill, the Mainers crossed the mill race   **Two siege guns at Chatham**
and tramped "over fences and obstructions of all   **Manor typify the federal**
kinds," walking across dead and wounded Yankees.   **artillery deployed at**
Fredericksburg. (bfs)

"On we pushed, up slopes slippery with blood"
and left muddy from earlier charges, Chamberlain
said. As darkness fell, the Maine boys "reached that
final crest" below the stone wall and "exchanged
fierce volleys" with the almost hidden Confederates.
Shooting continued "until the muzzle-flame deepened
the sunset red, and all was dark," he recalled.

The temperature plummeted, and a cold north
wind shivered the living. Shooting gradually ended,
but no Yankee dared stand; many Northerners, in
fact, stacked dead bodies into rude windbreaks and
hunkered down for the night.

Ames and Chamberlain set pickets, but the
Confederates did not come. The lieutenant colonel
lay down behind two dead men and pulled "another
crosswise for a pillow." Then he pulled "the [man's
coat] flap over my face" to fend off the chilling winds.
"Once a rough but cautious hand lifted the dead
man's coat-flap from my face, and a wild, ghoul-like
gaze sought to read whether" Chamberlain was alive.

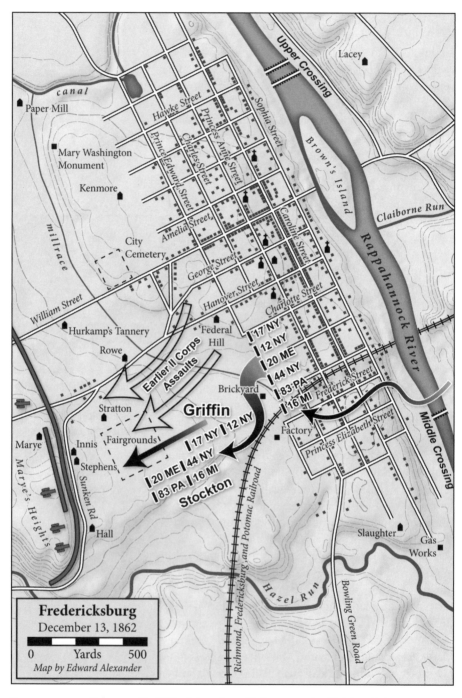

Fredericksburg
December 13, 1862

0   Yards   500
Map by Edward Alexander

FREDERICKSBURG, DECEMBER 13, 1862—Advancing with its parent 1st Division, V Corps, the 20th Maine and Lt. Col. Joshua Chamberlain crossed the Rappahannock River and deployed to charge Marye's Heights. The division was pinned down as darkness fell over Fredericksburg. A 7-Eleven now occupies the approximate spot where the regiment spent the night on the field.

Smoke rises from burning buildings as Union artillery shells Confederate infantry holding Fredericksburg. (loc)

His sleep disrupted by the verbal agony rising over the body-strewn slope, he and 20th Maine Adjutant John M. Brown sought to aid the wounded. The perceptive Chamberlain sorted the "monotone" into its disparate elements: men expressing "inarticulate agony," lifting prayers heaven-ward, begging for water, calling out relatives' names. "We did what we could, but how little it was," primarily providing rudimentary first aid or trickling water into dying soldiers' mouths. Finally, the "ghostly ambulances" came up on the lower slopes and started removing the wounded.

Along the 20th Maine lines, the "unmurmuring" wounded received medical care, and Chamberlain understood their silence. A bedrock Maine Yankee like them, he had inherited "that old New England habit so reluctant of emotional expression," a taciturn trait he overcame with Fanny and his postwar writings.

New York engineers build a pontoon bridge as Union infantrymen arrive to occupy Confederate-held Fredericksburg. (loc)

The wind "roared" all night and set a window blind to flapping "in a forsaken brick house to our right," he recalled after returning to his bivouac among the dead. Wounded by "a spent ball" that struck his right ear and neck, the exhausted Chamberlain finally fell asleep.

His men spent Saturday behind a corpse breastworks Ames had "ordered . . . to be thrown up." About 11:00 p.m., a regiment sent by Brig. Gen. Samuel D. Sturgis (2nd Division in IX Corps) relieved the 20th Maine men, who evacuated their wounded

A modern street extends from intown Fredericksburg toward Marye's Heights on the horizon. (bfs)

to Fredericksburg, reaching the ruins "cold, wet, and battle-worn" early on Monday, December 15.

Overhead, "Heaven ordained a more sublime illumination," Chamberlain said while watching the Aurora Borealis cast "its marvelous beauty" above Fredericksburg. "Fiery lances and banners of blood, and flame, columns of pearly light, garlands and wreaths of gold—all pointing and beckoning upward. Befitting scene!"

Before Monday dawned, the 20th Maine was sent back to its former position about 200 yards from the Sunken Road. "The order was to 'hold that ground at all hazards,'" recalled Chamberlain. "We had been sent out to hold the front while our forces evacuated the city."

Daylight passed, night fell, and Ames ordered the three

The National Park Service reconstructed the Stone Wall in 2004. (bfs)

regiments temporarily under his command to wield "pick and spade" and dig in, Chamberlain said. Orders came about 4:00 a.m., Tuesday, to pull back, and the Maine boys quietly crossed a pontoon bridge to the Rappahannock's eastern shore.

Rain fell as Chamberlain led the regiment "up that bank." In the murky daylight, men turned and "looked back across at Fredericksburg, and saw the green slopes blue with the bodies of our dead."

Confederate infantrymen defend the stone wall below Marye's Heights. (loc)

All his remaining years, Chamberlain would honor the men, officers and rank-and-file alike, with whom he served during the war. At this particular moment, however, he noticed the 20th Maine's "flag, its blue shield rent in many places."

"Our men did not hesitate—did not retreat. I believe the regiment has done honor to its State and country," wrote Chamberlain, proud to be a Mainer.

Mud and Mutineers

CHAPTER THREE

DECEMBER 17, 1862 - JULY 2, 1863

Colonel Adelbert Ames and Lt. Col. Joshua Chamberlain brought the 20th Maine, minus the four men killed and 32 wounded at Fredericksburg, into winter camp at Stoneman's Switch, and weary soldiers built the rudimentary cabins they would call "home" until spring 1863. Few Mainers noticed when Maj. Gen. George G. Meade took over V Corps on Christmas Day.

Then came a strange order from Ambrose Burnside to Maj. Gen. Joseph Hooker (Center Grand Division). Dated December 26 and relayed via chief of staff Maj. Gen. John Parke, the order directed Hooker to send a division to Richards' Ford on the Rappahannock River's north branch. "If . . . practicable," a brigade would cross there and march up the Rappahannock to "return by Ellis' Ford."

Hooker tapped 1st Division, V Corps. With commander Brig. Gen. Charles Griffin unavailable, Col. James Barnes took the division upriver on Tuesday afternoon, December 30 "with three days' rations and a full supply of ammunition." The 1st U.S. Sharpshooters, Battery D of the 5th U.S. Artillery, and 12 ambulances went with Barnes. At Hartwood Church, he picked up a hundred 3rd Pennsylvania Cavalry troopers, and his 2nd Brigade and Battery D diverted toward Morrisville. The other brigades bivouacked near Richards' Ford at 11:00 p.m. "in a dense wilderness," recalled a 118th Pennsylvania soldier.

The summer sky plays above a Union cannon at Fairview on the Chancellorsville battlefield. (bfs)

New Year's Eve dawned "cold, dull," and the Union boys marched at 8:00 a.m. Barnes discovered only 8-10 troopers from the 1st South Carolina Cavalry "occupying a house near the river" at Richards' Ford. The 1st Sharpshooters fired on the Southerners, and Barnes sent his cavalry and the 1st Brigade across the ford.

Retreating Confederates briefly fired from "a fine old Virginia mansion, occupied by a farmer and his three daughters." Union infantry returned fire. A bullet struck one daughter in a thigh, a surgeon patched her up, and the Union expedition marched 6-7 miles to Ellis' Ford. Union cavalry crossing there from the opposite shore chased off South Carolinian pickets and soon ran into Barnes' column, which waded the cold Rappahannock about 3:00 p.m. Returning to Stoneman's Switch on January 1, 1863, the 20th Maine lads probably wondered what the reconnaissance had accomplished.

Best known for writing "Taps," Dan Butterfield received the Medal of Honor for his heroism at Gaines' Mill. (loc)

Hooker passed the expeditionary results to Parke, who wrote "nothing new here" in a December 31 note to Burnside, already thinking about an end run around Fredericksburg. He set the Army of the Potomac marching upriver, out of enemy sight (but not knowledge) on January 20 to cross the Rappahannock and Rapidan rivers and get behind Robert E. Lee. The day started warm, the roads dry. Torrential rain swept in late day, drenching men and beasts and glooping Virginia's red mud into quicksand texture.

The 20th Maine made three miles that Tuesday. The rain continued falling, the army bogged down, and the Maine boys corduroyed a road on January 23. Then Burnside gave up the "Mud March." The army turned around and slogged back to its camps.

Sacking Burnside on January 26, President Abraham Lincoln installed Hooker as army commander. He quickly tackled the rampant desertion and poor nutrition, fired some generals, and created badges "for the purpose of ready recognition of corps and divisions in this army."

John Parke relayed a strange order to Joe Hooker on December 29, 1862. (loc)

Brigadier General Seth Williams, assistant adjutant general, included badge sketches in the order issued on March 21. To I Corps went the sphere (circle), II Corps the trefoil (three-leafed clover), III Corps the lozenge (a diamond), and V Corps received the Maltese cross. Sixth Corps got the Greek cross,

XI Corps a crescent, and XII Corps a star. Within each corps, each division's badge took a patriotic color: red for the 1st Division, white for the 2nd, and blue for the 3rd. Assigned to the 1st Division, V Corps, Chamberlain and his men sewed red Maltese crosses atop their kepis. The 20th Maine boys now visually identified with something greater than their regiment: a division and a corps. That red Maltese cross would march into history with the 1st Division.

The Mud March contributed significantly to morale breakdown within the Army of the Potomac. (hw)

*   *   *

Chamberlain came home on a 15-day leave in early February, when snow lay deep in the woods and Mainers lingered near hearths and stoves. While visiting with his family, he went to Augusta to meet with Governor Abner Coburn, who was so unpopular with aspiring Maine Republican political powerhouse James G. Blaine that he picked a gubernatorial candidate to replace Coburn within a few months.

For reasons unclear, Coburn criticized the 20th Maine during the February meeting. Biting his tongue, Chamberlain hoped his regiment's "continued good conduct" would cause the governor to "have a better opinion of us than you were pleased to express to me." Maybe "the good name we hold in the army will before long reach our home in the state we honor," Chamberlain wrote after returning to Virginia and recommending to Coburn several candidates for promotion, including Sgt. Tom Chamberlain to second lieutenant. Whatever he felt about the 20th Maine, Coburn approved the promotions.

Abraham Lincoln raised Joe Hooker to army command after sacking Ambrose Burnside. (loc)

Some Maine regiments enjoyed good press and political relations, with uniformed correspondents filing pseudonymic reports with the local papers and sycophantic officers cozying up to powerful Maine politicians. Adelbert Ames focused on fighting and not stroking media or Maine State House egos. "We

The Fredericksburg ruins
stood bleak when viewed from
the Stafford County shore in
February 1863. (na)

employ no reporters—have no partizans at home—the papers do not load us with praise we do not deserve," Chamberlain had told Fanny. Instead ". . . in the Army & by Regular officers we are already said to be a marked Regt" sought by other generals for their brigades.

On April 12 Chamberlain applied for a five-day leave to travel to Washington and Baltimore to meet Fanny, recently arrived in the capital. Leaving the regiment on April 14, he relished the days with his wife, the last private time they would enjoy for months as the war heated up.

In late March, surgeons had inoculated the 20th Maine boys against smallpox by exposing them to the cow pox, a similar and milder virus. "By some blunder of the medical director, the small-pox was introduced," with the disease evident by April 17, and several men caught smallpox "in its most violent form," growled Pvt. Theodore Gerrish, Co. H.

Maine Governor Abner
Coburn held the 20th
Maine—and perhaps Joshua
Chamberlain—in low opinion.
(msa)

Army regulations confined the regiment on April 22 "on what was known as Quarantine hill," he said.

Working amidst the pouring rain that raised local rivers and hampered Chancellorsville-related cavalry operations, the 20th Maine lads got their new camp "into a tolerable compact heap," Chamberlain wrote Fanny on April 24. Troubled "that I may not be able to take part in the next fight," he described how "direful looking placards" marked "Small Pox" stood at each camp entrance. An April 27 addendum indicated that "we saw our Division & Brigade move, & we felt lonesome." Surgeons figured the quarantine would run "a fortnight at least," and Chamberlain wished Fanny "could be here now" so "I can endure it."

While touring the Maine units assigned to the Army of the Potomac, Governor Coburn reviewed the 20th Maine on April 27. The "short visit" apparently did not go well as Chamberlain later apologized that "I could not do more to make your stay agreeable."

The regiment would have stayed at Quarantine Hill had not Adelbert Ames "offered "his services as volunteer aid[e]" to major generals Meade and Hooker. Leaving Chamberlain in command, Ames rode away, never to rejoin the 20th Maine. Meade even cited him in dispatches.

Hearing the Chancellorsville cannonading on May 2, the antsy Chamberlain promptly rode to V Corps' headquarters. Put in the 20th Maine anywhere you want, he implored. "If we couldn't do anything else, we would give the rebels the small pox."

His die cast, Chamberlain returned to camp. That midnight brought an order from Maj. Gen. Dan Butterfield, Hooker's chief of staff, for the 20th Maine to reach Banks' Ford and United States (U.S.) Ford at daybreak on May 3 to guard "the signal and telegraph lines from headquarters" to the Signal Corps' stations on the battlefield. Butterfield told Chamberlain "to put to death any one" sabotaging the communications network.

Signal Corps soldiers string a telegraph line at Brandy Station. The smallpox-quarantined 20th Maine guarded miles of telegraph wire during the Chancellorsville campaign. (na)

The Signal Corps had already run a telegraph line to Banks' Ford, just above Fredericksburg. The line extended to U.S. Ford (located 10 miles farther upriver) on April 29 had incorporated "wire of doubtful character," and "it was laid with distrust" by signalmen, noticed J. William Brown of the Signal Corps.

Spreading 20th Maine detachments "from the United States Ford to Falmouth," Chamberlain told his men "to shoot any one caught tampering with the wire." His boys kept busy "as the wire was tampered with & broken many times a night," he reported. "I was in my saddle all the nights inspecting every inch of the line," which was often laid along the ground or strung through bushes or trees.

After capturing Hazel Grove during Chancellorsville, Confederates used artillery to pound Union guns at Fairview. (bfs)

While near Chancellorsville, Chamberlain finally found the combat he sought. About 3:00 p.m. on Sunday, May 4, Brig. Gen. Charles Griffin sent Col. James McQuade and his 2nd Brigade "to feel for the enemy" opposite the 1st Division's positions. McQuade pushed out half a mile, "driving in the enemy's pickets and skirmishers" and finding the main Confederate battle line. Chamberlain rode along on "the reconnaissance," and a Confederate shot and wounded Prince, his "white stallion," in the head. The stallion was among the few Union casualties; McQuade commented that his skirmishers, the 4th Michigan, advanced "so rapid and determined" that enemy skirmishers fled without returning "our fire effectively. To this I attribute the slight loss sustained during the skirmish" described later by Chamberlain as "Griffin's Charge."

The beaten Army of the Potomac withdrew across the Rappahannock, and headquarters released the 20th Maine from its telegraphic protection on Tuesday evening, May 6. The regiment got lost—and good and soaked—while tramping in the "darkness and rain" to Quarantine Hill.

The smallpox quarantine ended on May 15.

*   *   *

Two significant events affected Chamberlain on Wednesday, May 20. The War Department made Ames a brigadier and gave him the 1st Brigade, 2nd Division, XI Corps. With Ames and Griffin recommending him for the vacant colonelcy, Chamberlain took over the 20th Maine.

Early that morning, the 18th Massachusetts had escorted Col. George Varney and 274 officers and men of the 2nd Maine to Stoneman's Switch to catch a train to Aquia Landing. The regiment was mustering out. Left behind were 120 men who, perhaps by recruiters' sleight of hand, believed they had enlisted for two years while actually signing up for three. Thinking "they were to be mustered out"

Joshua Chamberlain rode along with James McQuade and his brigade during a Chancellorsville reconnaissance. (loc)

with the 2nd, a Boston reporter noted, "they have been much offended at the government holding them for another year. They will be transferred to the Maine 20th."

The men made noise and "refused to do military duty," Chamberlain commented. Considering them "mutineers," the army put them "in a prisoners' camp . . . waiting court-martial," and Secretary of War Edwin M. Stanton transferred them to the 20th Maine.

Ordering the 118th Pennsylvania to march the mutineers at bayonet point to the 20th Maine's camp on May 24, Meade instructed Chamberlain, "Make them do duty, or shoot them down the moment they refuse."

The lieutenant colonel immediately hied to V Corps' headquarters and got from Meade "permission to manage the men in his own way." Returning to camp, Chamberlain discovered the mutineers had not been issued rations for three days. He released the guards, had the 2nd Maine boys fed, placed them on the regimental rolls, and "distributed them by groups" across his 10 companies "to break up the 'esprit de corps'" the mutineers might have developed. Of the 120 mutineers, only six refused to join the ranks.

This striking 2nd Maine Infantry monument stands at Mount Hope Cemetery in Bangor, Maine. (bfs)

Chamberlain warned they would be treated as "soldiers" and not "as civilian guests." He would investigate "their claim," but three-year enlistees they were. Believing that recruiters had made "promises . . . not now kept," Chamberlain sympathized with the men. "They need to be managed with great care & skill."

The mutineers arrived just as Robert E. Lee started his army toward Pennsylvania. For Chamberlain and the 20th Maine, the Gettysburg campaign opened with a seven-mile evening tramp from Ellis' Ford to Morrisville on June 13.

Then the marching turned serious as Jim Barnes led the 1st Division north through torrid summer heat. The sweltering sun killed four men on June

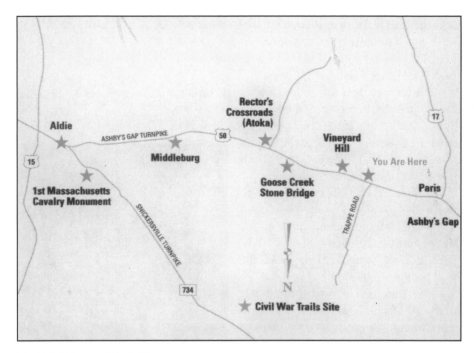

The 20th Maine participated in the July 21 fight that cleared Confederate cavalry from Middleburg, Virginia. (cwt)

17 and felled Chamberlain, who was left in Gum Springs as his men pushed north to Aldie. Too sick to command, he reached that town on June 21 as Union cavalry pried Jeb Stuart's cavalry from Middleburg to the west. The 1st Division added its heavy firepower, and the Confederates fell back to Upperville; the 20th Maine returned to Aldie the next day.

Representing the U.S. Christian Commission, Reverend John Chamberlain arrived unexpectedly at the 20th Maine's camp that evening, pleasantly surprising his brothers. John had traveled with Reverend Rowland Howard (brother to Maj. Gen. Oliver Otis Howard of XI Corps) on a mail wagon through "Mosby's Confederacy" to reach XI Corps. Brigadier General Adelbert Ames promptly sent John Chamberlain under armed escort to the 20th Maine.

Officially a colonel on June 23, Joshua Chamberlain rejoined his regiment that Tuesday and, still ill, stayed in the saddle as the Army of the Potomac hurried north to catch the Confederates now loose in Pennsylvania. The 3rd Brigade marched a rainy 20 miles on June 26 and pounded out 20 miles on June 27 to camp near Frederick, Maryland.

The V Corps paused on Sunday, June 28, as Meade took over the army and Maj. Gen. George

Sykes replaced him at corps command. Moving with V Corps early on June 29, the 3rd Brigade traipsed 18 miles, bivouacked, and added another 23 miles to camp at Union Mills on June 30.

Heading out at 11:45 a.m., Wednesday, July 1, the brigade made Hanover in midafternoon and camped as fighting raged at Gettysburg. With his positions there in a shamble, Meade hurled messengers to his senior commanders. At 6:00 p.m. Barnes received "orders . . . for an immediate resumption of the march." Tramping through the night, his divisions reached Gettysburg around 7 a.m., on Thursday, July 2.

"It is fifty-five miles from Frederick City to Gettysburg by the route they took," Chamberlain later calculated. Moving along rough roads while "weighed down with all the burdens of heavy marching order" and suffering from "the fiery heats of a midsummer sun," the 20th Maine boys were in good "physical condition," he thought.

A Mexican War veteran, George Sykes made the regular army his career. (loc)

Sometime between 4:00 p.m. and 5:00 p.m., orders came from Sykes for the 1st Division "to move toward the left and to the front," Barnes recalled. Forming into column, the division "moved rapidly up the Taneytown road," with Sykes and Barnes riding ahead. They scouted the terrain that the division must defend as the en echelon attack by James Longstreet and his First Corps shattered the III Corps of Maj. Gen. Daniel Sickles to the west.

With Barnes came three brigades. Col. Strong Vincent, a just-turned-26-years-old lawyer from Erie, Pennsylvania, led the 3rd Brigade. With it came the 83rd Pennsylvania, formerly commanded by Vincent and now led by Capt. Orpheus Saeger Woodward; the 16th Michigan of Lt. Col. Norval E. Welch; the 44th New York under Col. James C. Rice; and the 20th Maine.

The last regiment's acting major, Capt. Ellis Spear, watched as "one [shell] exploded in our column just in front of us." The attack against III Corps had started some time past, and now "stragglers and wounded men" visible along the Taneytown Road "indicated a severe struggle" off to the west.

That struggle was coming the 20th Maine's way.

$\mathcal{S}$tand-up $\mathcal{F}$ight at $\mathcal{L}$ittle $\mathcal{R}$ound $\mathcal{T}$op

CHAPTER FOUR

JULY 2 - JULY 5, 1863

Hurrying to help the disintegrating III Corps, the 1st Division of V Corps turned west off the Taneytown Road and tramped toward the Wheatfield. Based on the after-action report filed by Brig. Gen. James Barnes, the 3rd Brigade crossed Plum Run before Brig. Gen. Gouverneur K. Warren, the army's chief engineer, "came up, riding rapidly from the left (south)."

Gesticulating, Warren warned Sykes about Confederate infantry moving past III Corps' collapsing flank toward the hill "not far off and toward the left," Barnes recalled.

Can you spare some troops to defend the hill? Warren asked. Sykes agreed and told Barnes to send men. He in turn ordered Col. Strong Vincent and the 3rd Brigade to "proceed to that point."

Chamberlain recalled "a [Warren] staff officer" searching for Sykes and finding Vincent instead. "Taking the responsibility," Vincent marched for Little Round Top.

"We broke to the right and rear" and crossed Plum Run on "a rude log bridge," Chamberlain said. The 3rd Brigade ran along "a rough farm-road leading" to the peak, rocky along its western face, wooded on its northern slope, and partially wooded along its summit. The hill stood 670 feet above sea level and rose 63 feet above the saddle separating the hill from the taller, tree-covered hill to its immediate south.

Local residents called the shorter peak "Sugar Loaf

In 1886, 20th Maine survivors erected a utilitarian monument on Little Round Top. (bfs)

Joshua Chamberlain admired Strong Vincent for his courage and leadership. (loc)

Hill," "High Knob," and other names. Initially referring to the hill as "Granite Spur," Chamberlain dubbed it "Little Round Top" after his regiment fought there.

Captain Ellis Spear, Co. G, described Little Round Top as "more gently sloping" and "covered with open woods" along "the northern end, and the eastern slope, and scattered over with boulders."

The western slope resembled "a broken down wall of boulders, large and small," and dropped away "open and rocky," Spear noted. The brigade maneuvered south along "this wooded slope" and reached the south end of Little Round Top.

From the base and up the slope on both sides grew "oak trees, or chiefly with oak of perhaps a foot in diameter, more or less, with here or there a sprinkling of pines," Spear assessed the terrain. He particularly noticed that "the boulders were everywhere, some large and some small."

Confederate gunners zeroed on the brigade moving up Little Round Top. Bursting shells rained tree limbs and metal on the Yankees, noticed Chamberlain who was "riding abreast" with brothers John and Tom. "A solid shot" flew past their faces. "Boys, I don't like this. Another such shot might make it hard for mother," Chamberlain said, before sending John to find a field-station site and 1st. Lt. Tom, the acting adjutant, to the regiment's rear to "see that it is well closed up!"

Vincent placed the 16th Michigan, 44th New York, 83rd Pennsylvania, and 20th Maine from right to left (west to east) to defend the southern and western slopes. He stressed to Chamberlain that the Mainers held "the extreme left of the Union line.

"You understand! Hold this ground at all costs!" Vincent exclaimed before returning to the summit and death and glory.

The 3rd Brigade's line stretched in "nearly that of a quarter circle," the terrain "mostly . . . high rocks and cliffs on the center, and becoming more wooded and less rugged as you approached the left" flank, noticed Col. James Rice, soon to replace Vincent as brigade commander.

Chamberlain brought to Little Round Top 28 officers and 358 enlisted men, one-third of them the 2nd Maine mutineers foisted on the 20th Maine.

Issued 60 rounds apiece, the Maine boys lined up by company along the regimental perimeter.

From right to left, companies E, I, K, D, F, A, H, C, and G "formed that rugged line of battle among the crags and bowlders of that crest," Chamberlain said.

He ordered "the pioneers and provost guards . . . all but the drummer boys and hospital attendants" into the ranks. Three 2nd Maine hold-outs joined the fight, leaving only three recalcitrant mutineers later transferred to the brigade's provost guard.

Other 20th Maine soldiers, anywhere from three to at least a dozen per company, served elsewhere "on special duty or detached service," some with non-Maine artillery batteries, a few as teamsters, and others in the regimental hospital. Although Co. F was the color company this day, Sgt. Andrew Tozier of Company I was "detached" as "regt'l color-bearer."

Chamberlain examined the terrain in those last quiet minutes. "A smooth, thinly wooded valley" separated Little Round Top from Big Round Top, "a commanding summit," he noticed. His left flank in the air, Chamberlain sent Capt. Walter G. Morrill and his Co. B "as skirmishers . . . to the front and left." Crossing "the flat" between the Round Tops, Morrill and his men had "just commenced to ascend Big Round Top" when they heard "heavy volleys of musketry in our rear, where we had just left the regiment."

Abandoning Big Round Top, Morrill scurried his men "by the left flank" to find the Confederates. The Mainers moved east through the woods and reached a field nearer the Taneytown Road. Morrill encountered "some twelve to fifteen U.S. Sharpshooters" who, after protecting III Corps' left flank south of Houck's Ridge, had withdrawn before the advancing Confederates. When their "non-commissioned officer . . . asked leave to remain under my command," Morrill added the green-clad sharpshooters to his depleted company, which "took position behind the stone wall there" on the field's edge.

Along the 20th Maine's line, gunfire erupting to the west warned that approaching Confederate

Gouverneur K. Warren alternated between combat and engineer assignments before Gettysburg. (bfs)

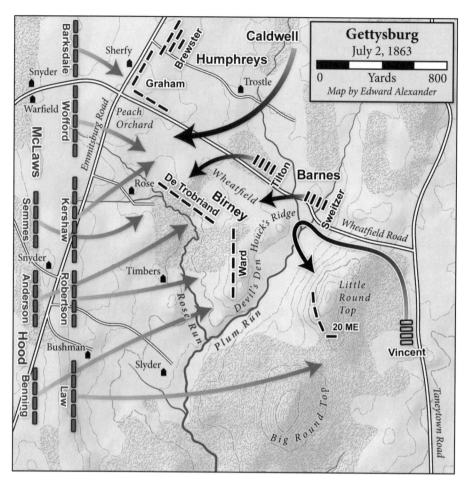

GETTYSBURG, JULY 2, 1863— Summoned by Gouverneur K. Warren, Strong Vincent swung his 3rd Brigade back across Plum Run and occupied Little Round Top as other Union units fought in the Wheatfield and along Houck's Ridge.

infantry now engaged the 16th Michigan, then the 44th New York, and finally the 83rd Pennsylvania. His all-Alabama brigade now reinforced by the 4th and 5th Texas, Brig. Gen. Evander McIver Law targeted the saddle between the Round Tops.

The 20th Maine had barely deployed "when the attack commenced," said Chamberlain. The enemy appeared in the saddle, and the right of the "Regt. found itself at once hotly engaged."

"The fire was hot" on the right flank, "but we gave them as good as we got," with the Confederates apparently trying "to cut us up by their fire," Chamberlain sensed in the opening 15 minutes or so.

With other Confederate regiments already engaging Vincent's 3rd Brigade, Col. William Calvin Oates took his 15th Alabama and the 47th Alabama toward the saddle. Union sharpshooters concealed on Big Round Top "poured an annoying fire" on the passing Confederates; Oates diverted uphill to dislodge the snipers, "who mysteriously disappeared."

He occupied the Big Round Top summit, but Law ordered the two regiments downhill to turn the Union left. Chamberlain later described the 15th and 47th as "the most formidable assailants of the Twentieth," and the 15th Alabama "largely outnumbered the Twentieth Maine."

The Alabamians came not "by way of the valley," but directly from undefended Big Round Top, he said. "Emerging from the woody side of Big Round Top, they burst through the bushes down the steep slope," realized the startled Spear, the 20th Maine's acting major. "I saw their legs first."

He watched the Confederates move steadily "to the left" as if "about to overlap and flank us. I went quickly" to Chamberlain "on the right" and "advised him to bend back two companies" to meet the threat.

But 1st Lt. James K. Nichols, Co. K, had apparently warned Chamberlain "something queer was going on" behind the nearest Confederates. Climbing onto "a high rock" for a better view, the colonel saw "a heavy force" behind "their principal line, moving rapidly . . . toward our left, with the intention, as I judged, of gaining our rear unperceived."

Relaying "our peril to but one or two officers," likely Spear and Co. E's Capt. Atherton W. Clark (the acting lieutenant colonel), Chamberlain ordered "the left wing" to form "a solid and steady line in a direction to meet the expected assault" and "the right wing [to] move by the left flank," the men "taking intervals of a pace or two." Its left flank now refused and "in outline resembling a horse-shoe, nearly," the regiment curved around that section of the hill, Chamberlain noticed.

The right-flank companies dueled with the Confederates below them as the left flank changed position. The large Confederate column "gained their desired point of attack . . . and rushed forward with an impetuosity," Chamberlain noted. The enemy infantrymen "emerging from their cover" hit "a firm and steady front," and "a strong fire opened at once from both sides."

"I can not remember which side opened fire first," Spear admitted. Possibly "the first volleys" discharged

Although only a captain, Atherton W. Clark served as the 20th Maine's lieutenant colonel at Gettysburg. (msa)

Also a captain, Ellis Spear served as the 20th Maine's major at Gettysburg. (bmpl)

Ellis Spear remembered the oak trees, some pines, and the boulders covering the eastern slope of Little Round Top. (bfs)

"practically simultaneous; perhaps we were a trifle ahead" because "the enemy was moving and we were standing on the defense and ready."

That corner of Little Round Top exploded. The "uproar of musketry, the cloud and smell of battle smoke, tense excitement with many men falling[,] but no shouting[,] but men loading and firing as fast as possible," Spear described the violence occurring along the 20th Maine's left flank.

He watched as individual Confederates "crept forward and took shelter behind boulders" and fired at the Mainers. The Alabamians "overshot us generally," Spear believed.

Fighting engulfed the entire 20th Maine line. Nearer the center where Chamberlain stood, Confederates got "within ten paces of our line" before Yankee volleys halted the advance.

"The two lines met, and broke and mingled in the shock" of "a struggle fierce and bloody beyond any that I witnessed," Chamberlain recalled. Fighting "swayed to and fro," with more Confederates than Yankees in sight at particular moments.

"Gradually forced back till we came against the great rocks between us and Hazlett's guns," the 20th Maine lads "rallied and repelled the fire" once and "twice again with terrible carnage," said Chamberlain.

"The fight was literally hand to hand" as "squads of the enemy broke through our lines." The opposing lines "rolled backward and forward like a wave," and when the Confederates pulled back, the Maine boys brought in wounded men, friend and foe alike.

His men shooting through their allotted 60 rounds, Chamberlain "sent several messengers" rearward to find

Acting adjutant Tom Chamberlain fought with the 20th Maine at Little Round Top. A third brother, Reverend John Chamberlain tended the wounded at a nearby field station. (msa)

ammunition and reinforcements, neither forthcoming. A lull developed; Maine boys slipped out "to gather ammunition and more serviceable arms, from the dead and dying on the field," Chamberlain said.

The Mainers grabbed whatever workable weapons they found, including Confederate firearms, and "their own rifles and their own bullets were turned against them" as "we met the enemy's last and fiercest assault," he noticed. The Maine boys particularly traded their War Department-issued Enfields for "better muskets." "We found [the Enfields] did not stand service well," Chamberlain commented.

When enemy "fire slackened a little on the left," Spear "walked along to the center." He noticed the thin line near the color guard, its members almost all down. Sergeant Andrew Tozier "had picked up a musket . . . and with his left arm about the colors[,] stood loading and firing, and chewing a bit of cartridge paper," Spear remembered.

Big Round Top looms above Union defenses on Little Round Top. (loc)

Chamberlain, too, peered through the "smoke, when the black cloud lifted for a moment." Tozier stood alone, the color guard and the nearest companies to his left and right "cut away." He "was defending his colors with bullet, bayonet and [rifle] butt, alone!"

Chamberlain immediately sent his brother, Tom, and an orderly, Sgt. Ruel Thomas, to find men and protect Tozier and the national colors. A messenger sent running to Capt. Orpheus Woodward of the 83rd Pennsylvania sought "a company to fill this perilous gap." Woodward could spare no men.

Ammunition ran out here and there along the line. "Half of the left wing already lay on the field," and the survivors seemed "scarcely more than a skirmish line," Chamberlain noticed. With the enemy "pouring on us a terrible fire" and "our gallant line withered and shrunk," he decided to attack.

"As a last desperate resort, I ordered a charge," wrote Chamberlain on July 6, his pen underlining the

Confederate infantry overran Devil's Den (center) and advanced across open ground to attack Little Round Top. The monument in the photo (lower-left) is to the 16th Michigan, part of the brigade line to the right of the 20th Maine. (bfs)

Hunkered behind a stone wall, Walter Morrill and his Co. B attacked Confederates driven back by the 20th Maine's right-wheel advance. (bmpl)

last word. "The word 'fix bayonets' flew from man to man. The click of the steel seemed to give new zeal to all," and "the men dashed forward with a shout," he recalled when the memories were fresh.

Hustling over to Spear, Chamberlain explained his plan. Spear must "start the movement" and keep the left flank pivoting to the right. As Chamberlain moved toward the color guard in his line's center, 1st Lt. Holman Melcher of Co. F asked permission to recover wounded Mainers.

"Yes, sir," Chamberlain replied. "Take your place with your company. I am about to order a 'right wheel forward' of the whole regiment."

Melcher stepped to the line as Chamberlain shouted, "Bayonet!" Standing alongside Tozier— "abreast with the colors"—he watched as "the left wing whirled the enemy's right out of the shelter of rocks."

On Little Round Top's southeastern slope, "the [20th Maine's] two wings came into one line again, and extending to the left, and at the same time wheeling to the right, the whole regiment nearly described a half circle," he remembered. His sword drawn and "Melcher . . . dashing in and right up to my side," he moved with Tozier and the colors.

The left-flank companies traveled "over the space of half a mile, while the right [flank] kept within the support of the 83rd. Penna.," Chamberlain recalled. The advancing Mainers hit "the enemy's first line," where Confederates "stood amazed, threw down their loaded arms and surrendered in whole companies." Southerners farther to the rear fired on the approaching Mainers.

Chamberlain plunged into the enemy. A Confederate officer, Lt. Robert Wicker, simultaneously "handed me his sword" with one hand while lifting a heavy "Colts' revolver in the other." Aiming his revolver at Chamberlain's head, Zwicker pulled the trigger, fired, and missed.

A Union sword tip at his throat, the Confederate surrendered, perhaps because he saw "Melcher + his squad coming down like tigers," thought Chamberlain. Otherwise Wicker might have shot him because "4 barrels were loaded" in the Southerner's revolver.

The 20th Maine made "an extended 'right wheel'" that, according to a map later provided to James Barnes by Col. James Rice, swept the Confederates off Little Round Top and through the woods crossed by modern Wright Avenue. Charging into the saddle, the Maine boys "cleared the front of nearly our entire brigade," Chamberlain noted.

His Co. B riflemen silent so far, Capt. Walter Morrill opened fire as he heard the charge take place. Retreating Confederates may have backed into Co. B; Union volleys tore into the enemy ranks as Morrill bellowed "loud commands to charge" to convince the Confederates "I had a large body of troops there."

A low granite stone identifies Co. B's position during the Little Round Top fight. (bfs)

Company B and other 20th Maine components pursued the Confederates fleeing toward Big Round Top. Morrill and his men climbed the hill until Southerners fired. He ordered Co. B to ground, then withdrew about 9:00 p.m. upon orders from Chamberlain.

With some 20th Maine troops shouting, "On the road to Richmond!," Chamberlain reined in his rambunctious survivors and had them round up prisoners and tend the wounded. Reinforcements arrived from the 3rd Division of Brig. Gen. Samuel Wylie Crawford. Up came "3,000 rounds of ammunition," sent by the new 3rd Brigade commander, the 44th New York's Col. James Rice, said Chamberlain. Strong Vincent had fallen mortally wounded early in the fight.

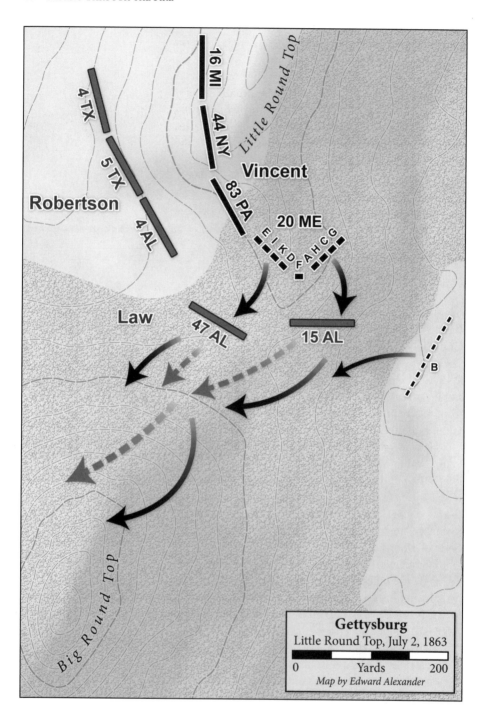

GETTYSBURG, LITTLE ROUND TOP, JULY 2, 1863—With his left flank refused and his men almost out of ammunition, Col. Joshua L. Chamberlain ordered a right wheel that ultimately straightened the regimental line and overran many Confederates attacking his position.

Confederate infantry faced a long climb up Little Round Top's open western slope. (bfs)

In one July 6 report, Chamberlain indicated that Rice arrived with the bullets and reinforcements. As "our dead [were] gathered and laid side by side," the two colonels apparently talked about the battle for Little Round Top. With Confederates lingering nearby, Rice asked Chamberlain to capture Big Round Top, which rose 785 feet above sea level.

Dusk found the 20th Maine survivors "worn out, and heated and thirsty," Chamberlain noticed. Men "had sunk down and fallen asleep" when the initial pursuit ended.

His heroes had captured 368 Confederates, "many of them officers," and had counted "at least" 150 dead or wounded enemy soldiers on Little Round Top. The 20th Maine had lost 136 men: 30 killed and 105 men wounded, "many mortally," and a man captured later that night, reported Chamberlain, wounded slightly in his right instep and bruised in the left thigh when a bullet struck his scabbard.

A marker indicates where the left flank of the 20th Maine stood during the height of the Little Round Top fight. (bfs)

"With bayonets fixed, the little handful of 200 men" pushed up Big Round Top around 9:00 p.m. The "steep and jagged" terrain broke up any semblance of a battle line, but Confederates uncertain as to how many Yankees thrashed uphill toward them fell back. Losing one lieutenant to an enemy bullet, the 20th Maine lads captured the summit and 25 Confederates. Southerners also scooped up one 20th Maine soldier as a prisoner.

The 83rd Pennsylvania (Chamberlain praised that regiment and Woodward), the 5th Pennsylvania Reserves, and the 12th Pennsylvania Reserves "came up and formed as a support" on Big Round Top that night, he reported.

The 1st Brigade of Col. William S. Tilton relieved the 20th Maine and the other regiments at noon on Friday, July 3. Chamberlain and his survivors shifted into position elsewhere.

The Little Round Top battle would enshrine the 20th Maine and Chamberlain in legend, bring the colonel a Medal of Honor in 1893, and generate controversy that echoes into the twenty-first century. While writing his infantryman's memoir in 1882, Theodore Gerrish (himself absent at Gettysburg) claimed that Holman Melcher initiated the charge. Standing near the color guard, he "saw the situation" and lunged "ten paces" toward the enemy. "With a cheer and a flash of his sword," he launched the charge while shouting, "Come on! Come on!"

The 20th Maine's right flank held tight against the 83rd Pennsylvania at Little Round Top. (bfs)

Over time after the war, the tale evolved to where Melcher is "now presented to the public as having suggested the charge," Chamberlain angrily wrote Ellis Spear 33 years after Gettysburg. "There is not truth in this. I had communicated with you" plans for the charge before Melcher asked permission to advance Co. F "and gather in some prisoners. There is a tendency now-a-days to make 'history' subserve other purposes than legitimate ones," Chamberlain growled.

But late in life, Spear would indirectly buttress Melcher, too, by repeating "the story as told by the men at the time and on the spot." Rather than crediting Chamberlain for ordering the charge, Spear claimed that Co. F soldiers anxious to recover wounded comrades outside the regimental line started crying, "Forward!"

The sword and scabbard worn by Joshua Chamberlain at Little Round Top are displayed at the Bangor Historical Society in Maine. (bhs)

The Co. F lads moved without Chamberlain's orders, companies on either side of Co. F thought the advance was officially sanctioned, away everybody went, and "it turned out excellently," commented Spear. No longer Chamberlain's friend by the early twentieth century, he did not mention his former colonel in this particular memoir, claimed no advance warning about the charge, and even called Strong Vincent "the true hero of Little Round Top (if any officer is to have that honor)."

Ironically, in 1885 Melcher credited Chamberlain with conceiving the charge and ordering the men "to 'fix bayonets.'" The regiment moved "almost before" the colonel could "say 'Charge!'" Melcher remembered.

As rain fell on Saturday, July 4, 1863, the controversies of memory still waited in the future. Brigadier General Charles Griffin rejoined the 1st Division and relieved Barnes. The 20th Maine reconnoitered out near Plum Run, found the enemy gone, and plodded through the murk to bury "our dead in the place where we had laid them during the fight," Chamberlain recalled.

Comrades erected a Strong Vincent monument at Little Round Top. (bfs)

Heat, humidity, and rain had disfigured the dead for 48 hours. Each fallen man went into the soil as well as his comrades could cover him. Survivors thrust into the soil by each hero's head "a head-board made of ammunition boxes, with each dead soldier's name cut upon it," Chamberlain reported.

His men also buried 50 Confederates found below where the regiment fought on July 2. Survivors checked on wounded comrades left in nearby houses and barns, and on Sunday morning, July 5, "we took up our march on the Emmitsburg road," Chamberlain said.

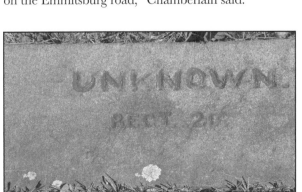

An unknown 20th Maine soldier lies at the National Cemetery in Gettysburg. (bfs)

Bird-Colonel Chamberlain Would Do

CHAPTER FIVE
JULY 6, 1863 - APRIL 1864

Breaking camp near Marsh Creek on July 6, Col. Joshua Chamberlain and the 20th Maine moved a mile nearer Emmitsburg, stopped, and bivouacked. Weary soldiers welcomed the rest; Chamberlain dealt with paperwork.

That Monday he wrote at least three after-action reports, one addressed to Brig. Gen. James Barnes (commanding the 1st Division), the second to 1st Lt. George B. Herendeen, the 3rd Brigade's acting assistant adjutant general. Not until November 4 did Chamberlain send this report with a cover letter to Maine Adjutant Gen. John L. Hodsdon. Also addressed to Herendeen, a third and lengthier July 6 report would become "No. 196" in the *Official Records, Volume 27*, published in 1889.

Pursuing the retreating Confederates, the 20th Maine marched 18-20 rainy miles to camp near Frederick, Maryland, on July 7 and crossed the Catoctin Mountains in a hellacious thunderstorm to bivouac near Middletown on Wednesday. The regiment crossed South Mountain via Crampton's Gap on Thursday as Maj. Gen. George Meade and the Army of the Potomac closed on Robert E. Lee, consolidating his Southerners at Williamsport.

On July 10 "I had command of our advance," Chamberlain recalled, and the 20th Maine lost one man killed and seven wounded while skirmishing with Confederates at Jones' Crossroad "on the Sharpsburg

An aqueduct carries the Chesapeake & Ohio Canal over Conococheague Creek at Williamsport, Maryland. (bfs)

Joshua Chamberlain wrote at least three separate Gettysburg reports on July 6, 1863. (msa)

& Hagerstown pike." The dead soldier was Pvt. Thomas Townsend, among the three 2nd Maine mutineers who while "awaiting trial took his gun & his place in the ranks" at Gettysburg, Chamberlain noted.

Trapped briefly at Williamsport, Lee pulled his army across the Potomac River on July 14. Pivoting to the southeast, V Corps moved through Maryland. The 20th Maine crossed into Virginia on July 17, and while writing Fanny that day from "Camp near Berlin, Md.," Chamberlain excitedly told her about what "my little scarred & battle-stained band" had accomplished at Gettysburg.

Proud that "the 20th held the post of honor on the extreme left of the whole army," he detailed the regiment's stand at Little Round Top and capture of Big Round Top, "an achievement which Gen [George] Sykes said was one of the most important of the day. & for which I rec[eive]d the personal thanks of all my commanders." As Chamberlain, now mounted, had led the 20th Maine "from the field," Col. James Rice "took me by the hand, & said "Col. C. your gallantry was magnificent, & your coolness & skill saved us."

Buoyed by such praise, Chamberlain took his men into Virginia and witnessed the noisy July 23 battle of Wapping Heights. Struggling physically since sun-struck a month earlier, he stayed in the field, but on July 27 he sought a 20-day leave "for reasons of my health" after his malaria recurred.

Chamberlain "had a severe attack of illness during the recent campaign," but had refused to step down "while in the face of the enemy." Now he would suffer "the most serious consequences" if he could not recuperate.

Charles Griffin commanded the so-called "West Point Battery" at First Bull Run. (loc)

Leaving the 20th Maine at Warrenton on July 31, he sought medical care in the capital, then caught a train to begin his 15-day leave in Maine. The sweet days with Fanny, Daisy, and Wyllys ended when Jim Rice, commanding the 3rd Brigade, wrote asking that Chamberlain return to Virginia so Rice could visit his wife, Josephine, in New York.

Chamberlain rejoined the 3rd Brigade as its temporary commander on August 20. The 1st Division's commander, Maj. Gen. Charles Griffin, replaced Rice (promoted to brigadier on August 23) with Chamberlain. When "general officers . . . were sent to him for assignment" to the 3rd Brigade, Griffin turned them away; bird-colonel Chamberlain would do.

He and other 20th Maine survivors vividly remembered Saturday, August 29, when V Corps formed a hollow square to see five deserters (all draftees) from the 118th Pennsylvania shot. Clergy lingered in prayer with the doomed men, each sitting upon his open coffin, and a 50-soldier firing squad stood waiting. Ten shooters faced each deserter.

Orders had scheduled the execution "between 12 noon and 4 p.m." Checking his watch long into the developing horror, Griffin suddenly yelled, "Shoot those men or after ten minutes it will be murder!" Fifty rifles soon volleyed from "within six paces," and the deserters died.

* * *

The V Corps formed to witness the August 29, 1863, execution of five deserters from the 118th Pennsylvania. (loc)

The days in Brunswick partially restored Chamberlain, warmly thinking about Fanny and "my little dear ones . . . all nestled together—'all'— I paused over that word" as a bugler sounded lights out one late August evening. Cherishing his family, he recalled hearing Fanny and Daisy pray for him, and he knew they did so every night. And no matter his situation, whether "on some perilous duty" or "in peril of forgetting God & his goodness," he believed "that [nightly] prayer has been heard for me."

He longed for Fanny. "Come & let me kiss your dear lips—precious wife—sad mother," and if only the war would end, "he hoped they could "only meet at last, as I pray God we may, never to part."

The V Corps crossed the Rappahannock River into Culpeper County in mid-September, spent some weeks camped near Culpeper, and then started tramping northeast along the Orange & Alexandria Railroad on October 13. Outflanking Meade, the Army of Northern Virginia raced to slip between the Army of the Potomac and Washington, D.C. The Yankees ultimately won the foot slog and the battle of Bristoe Station; enemy artillery found the 3rd Brigade's bivouac, and everyone was back along the Rappahannock within days.

Chamberlain noticed a particular captured horse that October. Described as small, with "mixed Morgan and Lexington blood," the horse displayed sores "from use as a pack animal." Paying the federal government $150 (a horse's going price), Chamberlain brought the horse to camp and restored him to health and vitality. Named Charlemagne, the horse soon displayed a "glossy" chestnut coat and a "mane and tail of a slightly darker hue."

The 3rd Brigade now camped near Warrenton Junction. Down the railroad at Rappahannock Station, Lee left a fortified bridgehead defended by artillery and 2,000 soldiers from Maj. Gen. Jubal Early's division.

Meade ordered the position taken. Major General John Sedgwick (VI Corps) deployed Maj. Gen. Albion P. Howe's 2nd Division outside the Confederate earthworks on Saturday, November 7. As it happened, the 6th Maine held Howe's left flank along the O&A Railroad tracks separating VI Corps from V Corps.

Just over the railroad bed, the 20th Maine held the right flank of Chamberlain's 3rd Brigade. Captain Walter Morrill and Co. B stood nearest the tracks; Mainers got to talking, and when Howe's infantry suddenly charged the bridgehead as planned after dark, Morrill and some 50 "volunteers" from the 20th Maine went in with the 6th Maine and helped overwhelm the surprised defenders.

Morrill received the Medal of Honor for leading his men that night. Chamberlain counted four men

The Rappahannock River flows past the former Rappahannock Station, where some 2,000 Confederates defended redoubts in early November 1863. (bfs)

killed and 16 wounded in the 3rd Brigade and pleasantly reported receiving "70 prisoners, including 5 officers." He did not mention that Charlemagne suffered a wounded foreleg, a harbinger of things to come.

The 1st Division probed across the Rappahannock River on November 8 and re-crossed to the Union shore the next day. Lacking firewood or shelter tents, Chamberlain and his men slept on hard ground; after dark on November 10, pelting sleet cooled into snowy shrouds covering the sleeping soldiers.

His malaria flaring on November 15, Chamberlain dictated a two-line request for a 15-day leave and enclosed a "Surgeon's Certificate" from Dr. Morris W. Townsend, surgeon for the 44th New York and chief surgeon, 3rd Brigade. "Dangerously sick," Chamberlain might die if transported by ambulance or hospitalized in the field, Townsend certified "on [my] honor."

Loaded into a cattle car, Chamberlain occasionally slipped unconscious as he rattled up the railroad with "some staff" and a doctor. He went to the Seminary General Hospital in Georgetown.

Fanny arrived to help care for her husband. The Chamberlains returned to Brunswick for Christmas and New Year's. Restless to return to duty, the colonel accepted assignment to courts martial in New Jersey and Washington, D.C. in February.

Union soldiers captured the Confederate fortifications at Rappahannock Station on November 7, 1863. (hw)

Returning to the capital, Fanny looked after him as the malaria recurred. In April 1864, the Chamberlains visited Gettysburg; Fanny listened and learned as Joshua led her across the 20th Maine's battleground on Little Round Top.

Joshua Chamberlain and his wife, Fanny, explored Washington, D.C. in winter 1864. (loc)

While serving on a Trenton, New Jersey "General Court Martial," Chamberlain applied to rejoin the army on April 25. That paperwork vanished, so he reapplied on May 9. "My anxiety to be in the field is very great," he wrote.

Already losing officers faster than they could be replaced, the army approved his request.

The Death Angel Could Not Claim Him

CHAPTER SIX
MAY 17 - JUNE 18, 1864

With enemy "shells . . . bursting over us every second" on Wednesday, May 18, 1864, Col. Joshua Chamberlain tucked into the Spotsylvania County soil and wrote a chatty letter to Maine's newest governor, Samuel Cony.

Rejoining V Corps and the 1st Division a day earlier, Chamberlain had temporarily replaced the ill Brig. Gen. Joseph J. Bartlett as 3rd Brigade commander. Tuesday evening "we advanced our lines half a mile . . . with little loss" near Spotsylvania Court House. Now the brigade lay "in the line of battle behind our rifle pit works not more than 600 or 800 yards from the enemy's works," he noted.

Cony could receive no fresher report from any battlefield.

His puppeteer's fingers pulling the Republicans' marionette strings in Maine, Congressman James G. Blaine had orchestrated replacing Governor Abner Coburn on the fall 1863 ballot with Cony. An Augusta native, Old Town lawyer, and Democrat-turned-Republican only in 1862, he won election and took office in early January 1864.

All business when under fire, Chamberlain recommended several "officers for promotions" in the 20th Maine and reported his difficulty in rejoining the regiment. "The week of active operations when I was kept out of the field was one of the most unhappy of my life.

"I am making up for it now" as "we have been exposed to a heavy cannonading all the morning," he

Battery 5 is located a short walk behind the Eastern Front Visitor Center at Petersburg National Battlefield. (bfs)

New York lawyer Joseph
Bartlett proved himself a
capable and courageous
wartime commander. (bmpl)

commented. "The artillery fire is very hot," and "the Brigade is losing men fast."

Twenty-four hours back in the saddle, and Chamberlain already knew "we . . . are moving to turn his [Robert E. Lee's] right & that of course brings us nearer to Richmond."

*   *   *

After Bartlett rejoined the 3rd Brigade, Chamberlain got the new 1st Brigade of the 1st Division (Brig. Gen. Charles W. Griffin) on June 6. This "splendid" brigade comprised six Pennsylvania infantry regiments: the 121st, 142nd, 143rd, 149th, 150th (veterans all), and the 187th, a "splendid new regiment," Chamberlain said. Taking charge of the "somewhat disheartened" Pennsylvanians "after Cold Harbor," he "set to work to restore their spirit."

The brigade participated in the Ulysses S. Grant-planned side slip to the James River. At Windmill Point on the morning of June 16, some regiments boarded the steamer Exchange, and the 187th Pennsylvania lads crammed aboard the tugboat *Eliza Hancock*.

The 1st Brigade disembarked at Guiney's Landing. Promptly issued soap and ordered into the water, Chamberlain's filthy soldiers liberally soaped up their uniforms, swam to wash off the suds and grime, and repeated the process before stepping ashore to dry beneath the hot sun. The last V Corps elements landed, the divisions reformed, and corps commander Maj. Gen. Gouverneur K. Warren started his men toward the army's far left flank at Petersburg.

A hiking trail crosses the
fields near the Bloody Angle at
Spotsylvania Court House. (bfs)

Replica Confederate cannons point toward the former Union lines at the Cold Harbor Visitor Center. (bfs)

"The road was rough and great clouds of dust covered the moving column," recalled James Gibbs of the 187th. After a short rest at sunset, the men marched "far into the night," pausing only "for a little while" to eat supper before resuming "the terrible march."

Lieutenant Colonel Horatio Warren of the 142nd Pennsylvania remembered the tramp as "the dustiest march we ever experienced." The dust clouds "nearly suffocated men and horses every step of the way." Not until long after dark did V Corps stop. Numbering "2,500 to 3,000 men," the 1st Brigade bivouacked "before the outer works of Petersburg" late on June 17, Chamberlain said.

That evening he suddenly experienced "a strange feeling . . . a premonition of coming ill." Familiar with malaria's warning signs, Chamberlain realized he was not sick. Spending considerable time walking "through the ranks of my silent or sleeping men," he reached his tent in "an unaccustomed mood."

"A shadow seemed to brood over me, dark wings folding as it were . . . and wrapping me in their embrace," Chamberlain recalled. He sensed or heard a voice: "Something said; 'You will not be here again. This is your last.'"

"The premonition became oppressive, unbearable," and, leaving the tent, he said good-bye to "some of my most intimate friends."

Most heard no grand finale in Chamberlain's tone, but Charles Griffin stirred when, after telling his night-owl brigade commander to "turn in and go to sleep," Chamberlain shared his presentiment.

"General, this is my last night with you," he said.

"What do you mean?" Griffin responded loudly.

"I shall fall tomorrow, General; this is my good-bye," Chamberlain explained.

"Why do you think so?" Griffin asked.

"The dark angel has said it to me," Chamberlain replied.

The friends talked briefly before parting.

*   *   *

Fifth Corps went forward Saturday morning and discovered the Confederates had pulled back in the night. Griffin worried about a few exposed Union batteries, and Chamberlain brought up the 1st Brigade behind them.

But enemy artillery across the way pounded at V Corps, and in his brigade "many were falling, with no chance to strike back; and this is hard to bear," Chamberlain noticed while riding Charlemagne along the brigade front. Then, Griffin and Warren rode over and asked if the 1st Brigade could chase away the Southern batteries on a nearby crest.

Away went the brigade, not in what Griffin believed would be "a hard push up that open slope," but to the left flank, concealed by the terrain until the Pennsylvanians reached "a piece of woods" on the right flank of the Southern gunners, Chamberlain recalled.

But he and Griffin rode straight toward the enemy artillery until discovering "a deep railroad cut" (belonging to the Norfolk & Petersburg Railroad) well-covered by Confederate cannons. Rejoining his brigade, Chamberlain took it across the tracks "at level grade" and up "a rough track" into the woods.

His men advancing in two lines, he led "the whole staff, flag flying aloft" fast toward the Southern gunners. Someone swung and fired a cannon; the bursting shell wounded Charlemagne and knocked down Chamberlain and "every one of my staff" and "my red Maltese cross," the brigade flag. "Enfilading fire from great guns on our left" pounded the charging brigade as its target fired a few canister rounds, limbered up, and skipped merrily over the hill's crest.

Chamberlain still lived.

While the brigade's pioneers dug and leveled artillery lunettes "just under the crest," either "Griffin or Warren" ordered out three artillery batteries—the 9th

Massachusetts Battery of Capt. John Bigelow; Battery C, 1st New York Light Artillery under Capt. Almont Barnes; and the 15th Battery, New York Light Artillery of Capt. Patrick Hart—to support Chamberlain.

Chamberlain recalled that his men helped the gunners roll their cannons "up into the places . . . made for them," with the gun muzzles situated "in the grass close to the earth," Chamberlain recalled. The cannons could help beat off counterattacks; two Pennsylvania regiments deployed to guard the brigade's exposed left flank, and Chamberlain set about "strengthening our position."

He expected no additional advancing that day. Then, an unidentified staff officer "much excited with his difficult journey" delivered an order from "either Meade or Grant" for the 1st Brigade to attack and capture the nearby Confederate earthworks.

Protesting the order to attack "the main works at Petersburg" unsupported, Chamberlain scribbled a letter detailing his tactical situation and requesting clarification as to the original order.

Noting that he had "carried a crest, an advance post occupied by the enemy's artillery, supported by infantry," Chamberlain placed his "isolated position" one mile "beyond our own lines." His left flank hung

Horse-drawn pontoon boats roll across a wharf and aboard a steamer moored at Windmill Point on the James River in mid-June 1864. (hw)

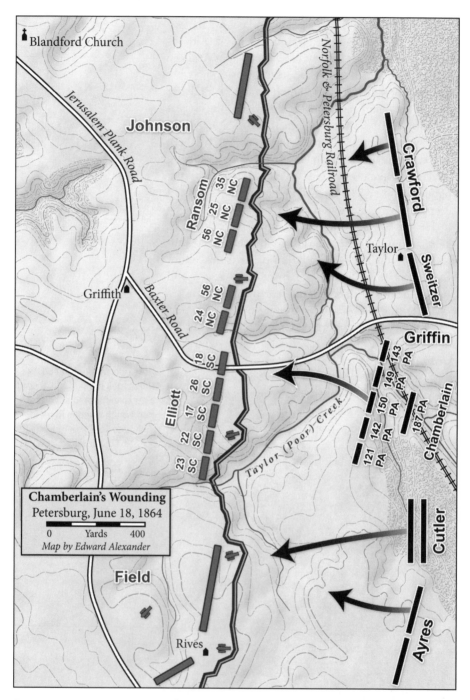

CHAMBERLAIN'S WOUNDING: PETERSBURG, JUNE 18, 1864—After helping push Confederate troops into their main defenses earlier on June 18, 1864, Col. Joshua L. Chamberlain received a questionable order to attack the enemy's main line in mid-afternoon. Assured that other units would support his brigade, he essentially advanced alone.

Taylor (Poor) Creek and its steep banks were natural obstacles to V Corps' troops advancing against Confederate lines on June 18, 1864. (bfs)

"in the air," and "a deep railroad cut" existed near his right flank. Confederate earthworks "with projecting salients right and left" rose "in my front at close range," he wrote. Chamberlain saw the embrasures for cannons; he knew that infantry hovered alongside the artillery.

Between his brigade and the enemy earthworks lay a "hollow . . . close up to the enemy's works." A visual reconnaissance detected in the hollow the "bad ground, swampy, boggy," the terrain that would naturally slow his men while "under a destructive fire." Off to the left flank "a large fort . . . enfilades my entire advance," and if the 1st Brigade attacked, the three Union batteries would be "unsupported, their retreat cut off by the railroad" if he suffered "repulse," noted Chamberlain, seeking assurance "that the order to attack with my single brigade is with the General's full understanding.

The old Baxter Road runs alongside Taylor (Poor) Creek at Petersburg National Battlefield. (bfs)

"If an assault is to be made, it should be by nothing less than the whole army," he opined.

The terrain described by Chamberlain and other 1st Brigade survivors corresponds significantly to the brushy, tree-studded ravine created by Taylor Creek (also called "Poor Creek"), crossed by the Baxter Road, its wartime route still visible today. Some Union officers would cite the ravine's steep banks, up which soldiers must clamber before taking the cold steel to the enemy earthworks lurking on higher ground.

The staff officer (a colonel) rode off with Chamberlain's letter and returned a while later. "The whole army will attack" while guiding on the 1st Brigade, he reported. Other units needed time to prepare.

"I will attack at 3 o'clock," Chamberlain said, after comparing time with the colonel. High command supposedly alerted the participating brigades.

Years later Chamberlain described his target as "Rives' Salient," which "completely commanded" the terrain that his brigade must cross. He placed the "strong earthworks" only 300-400 yards away, "and just across the [Jerusalem] Plank Road [on the left] was a large fort (Fort Mahone) with heavy guns ready to sweep the crest we were occupying."

The attack "must be a storm of cannonade, a rush of infantry with pieces at the shoulder. Over the works and bayonet the enemy at their guns!" he thought. "It was desperate, deadly business."

Chamberlain formed his brigade in two lines, the 150th Pennsylvania out

Walnut Hill Elementary School stands on the site of Confederate-held Fort Mahone. (bfs)

front as skirmishers, the four other veteran regiments constituted the first line, and the large 187th, "numbering about 850 men," brought up the rear, Horatio Warren recalled. Chamberlain "and his staff would be between the two lines," Warren said. Some survivors placed Chamberlain on the far right, but his men knew he went with them.

His watch ticking to 3:00 p.m. Chamberlain briefed his regimental commanders, discussed targets with the three battery captains, and waited. He particularly warned his two senior colonels that "I resolved to lead the charge in person" and expected not to survive.

His watch's "minute hand" reached "the mark for 3 o'clock," and "I told the bugler to sound the 'charge.'"

"Up rose my brave men; past the batteries they press . . . down the slope they go; muskets on the shoulder; bayonets fixed," said Chamberlain. The Confederates across the way "opened with every kind of missile man has invented."

Glancing to his right, Chamberlain realized that Union support had not materialized. Down went his dying flag-bearer, "the musketry was like a boiling sea," and solid shot and shell "sent the turf and stones through our ranks."

Now he carried the brigade flag, the red Maltese cross on the white field. Encountering "the borders of a marsh or bog," Chamberlain "made a half face to the left" and commanded, "'Incline to the left. To the left.'" His men could not hear him over the noise. Chamberlain "raised the flag . . . high as I could" and waved it while gesturing with his saber "towards the left . . . signaling 'To the left. To the left.'"

Suddenly he "felt a sharp hot flash that seemed to cut the spinal marrow out of my backbone." He thought fragments of an exploding shell had struck him, but a minié ball had punctured his right pelvis.

Lowering his flag staff and saber so he could lean on them, Chamberlain watched "my new noble regiment," the 187th Pennsylvania, advance past him. Then "hot blood" gushed in "my sword hand," and he saw blood "spurting out of my right hip-side." Blood slopped from his filled cavalry boot and out of "my baggy reinforced trousers."

"I sank first to my knees, then leaning on my right elbow," he recalled. Up came two aides who received

A Virginia Department of Historic Resources sign stands approximately where a Confederate bullet struck Joshua Chamberlain on June 18. (bfs)

Tom Chamberlain grabbed two army surgeons and searched the field hospitals to find his wounded brother. (phcc)

his last orders, and Chamberlain now lay on his back, his blood pooling beneath him, "more blood than the books allow a man."

The Death Angel had found him.

Chamberlain apparently looked dead, especially to "some men standing over me" discussing "with low-toned voices . . . what to do" with the colonel's body they had been sent to retrieve. Then "I spoke to them," he recalled, and "they brightened up."

The artillery lunettes indirectly saved his life, thanks to John Bigelow. "The infantry are swarming back through the line, and it looks like a repulse," noticed Levi Baker of the 9th Massachusetts Battery. "Our guns are getting hot; they are recoiling down the hill, but we run them to the front every time, and hold our position." He commanded "the right gun" in the rightmost two-gun section, overseen by Bigelow. The hill's crest protected the gunners as they reloaded, but pushing a cannon into its rough embrasure spelled danger; shot in the mouth, a gunner at the No. 2 gun fell backwards while sighting his cannon.

Venturing amidst fleeing 1st Brigade stragglers, Bigelow and Lt. R. S. Milton rounded up "over 100" soldiers and "made them lay down and load up." Then Bigelow learned that Chamberlain was down.

"I sent . . . to the ambulance to take the stretcher and bring him in, my informant acting as guide," Bigelow said. The stretcher bearers rushed across explosion-churned terrain to reach Chamberlain.

He urged them to rescue someone with a chance to live. Despite his protestations, the soldiers "put me on their stretcher, and started" up the incline the 1st Brigade had charged down. His rescuers had traveled "not 20 yards away" from where Chamberlain lay when a Fort Mahone-fired cannonball struck "the very spot" and dug "a grave large enough for all of us."

Setting down their patient, "a limp mass of bloody earth," behind the artillery, the soldiers soon loaded him into an ambulance that "galloped through rough stumpy fields" to the 1st Division's field hospital in "a cluster of pines" three miles away.

Hospital orderlies placed Chamberlain on an improvised table, and two surgeons—doctors W. R. DeWitt Jr. and R. A. Everett—ran a ramrod "through my body" to probe the wound and find the minié ball. Its conical point split into a vee, it jutted "with a puff of skin just behind my left hip joint." The ramrod's angle indicated that "the ball entered the right hip in front of and a little below the right trochanter major, diagonally backward," and exited "above and posteriorly to the left great trochanter." The ball severed blood vessels and nicked the urethra; urine mingled with blood seeping from the hole in Chamberlain's right hip.

The surgeons cut out the ball, dressed the incision, and bandaged the entrance wound. The orderlies placed Chamberlain "gently . . . on a pile of pine boughs," amidst other seriously wounded officers.

Along with Tom Chamberlain, Ellis Spear stood watch over the shattered Joshua Chamberlain. (loc)

Lengthening shadows indicated a lowering sun when Chamberlain saw several surgeons standing nearby, occasionally looking his way as they quietly discussed who should tell their patient the bad news. Finally, Chamberlain signaled one surgeon to join him and said, "It is a mortal wound. I know this, and am prepared for it."

"Yes, there is no possible chance for you," the surgeon responded. "You can not live till morning."

His fate ascertained, Chamberlain used a pencil to write "My Darling wife. I am lying mortally wounded the doctors think, but my mind & heart are at peace. Jesus Christ is my all sufficient savior. I go to him. God bless & keep & comfort you, precious one, you have been a precious wife to me." Mentioning his children, parents, sister, and brother John, Chamberlain signed off.

Friends, including Joseph Bartlett and Charles Griffin, visited him beneath "a lurid, wild, cloud-driven sunset." He reminded Griffin about the nocturnal June 17 premonition, and Griffin said that Grant had verbally promoted Chamberlain to brigadier. His shoulders heaving in the gathering dark, Griffin left.

*   *   *

Sometime later "a flood of tearing agony" shook Chamberlain, who "never dreamed what pain could be and not kill a man outright." He gradually slid "into a stupor," disrupted only when "through the mists" he saw Dr. Abner O. Shaw, 20th Maine, and Dr. Morris W. Townsend, 44th New York.

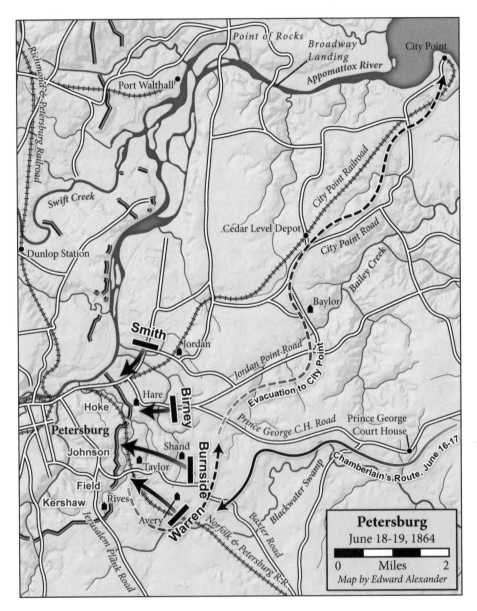

PETERSBURG, JUNE 18-19, 1864—When an army surgeon reported that Joshua Chamberlain could not survive evacuation by ambulance to City Point, George G. Meade authorized sending eight soldiers to carry the wounded colonel by stretcher. Chamberlain remembered the heat and the glaring sun encountered during the long trek.

They came with Capt. Tom Chamberlain, the often historically maligned younger brother who, with the surgeons in tow, scoured the field hospitals after learning that Joshua had been shot. The doctors "sat down by me" and used a medical instrument to probe for the severed blood vessels from which Chamberlain's life slowly ebbed.

Shaw and Townsend struggled with "the ever impossible task," Chamberlain recalled. Townsend finally told Shaw, "It is of no use, Doctor; he cannot be saved."

"Just once more, Doctor," replied Shaw. "Let me try this once more, and I will give it up."

This time Shaw "touched the exact lost thread; the thing was done," Chamberlain remembered. "There was a possibility . . . that I might be there to know in the morning."

Throughout the surgical intervention, "Tom stood over me like a brother." Next to him stood "true-heart [Ellis] Spear," both men "watching there like guardians over a cradle amidst the wolves of the mountain."

City Point separates the Appomattox River (left) and the James River. (bfs)

Late that night, Spear knelt and with a tin dipper fed porridge to Chamberlain. With "the tears . . . running down his cheeks" and "his red beard" illuminated by "a lurid campfire," Spear got the nourishment into his former regimental commander. "Taken all together, it was a good porridge," Chamberlain remembered.

He saw the dawn on Sunday, June 19. The United States Military Railroad had not yet reached out that far from City Point, so for Chamberlain that meant "a stretcher and 8 men to carry me the 16 miles to City Point," where a hospital ship would ferry him to the Army hospitals at Annapolis, Maryland.

Acting with "kind thoughtfulness," George G. Meade had sent the stretcher bearers, designated

Stretcher bearers carried Joshua Chamberlain aboard the hospital transport *Connecticut* at City Point. (loc)

"my 'forlorn hope'" by Chamberlain. "Griffin had been stirring," he said, believing his evacuation "was probably Griffin's doing" by badgering Meade.

Why detail men to carry Chamberlain so far? "The nature and severity of his wound would not admit his riding in an ambulance," *New York Herald* correspondent L. A. Hendrick learned.

Chamberlain's "condition from a pelvic wound rendered transportation by stretcher necessary," explained Townsend, detailed to accompany Chamberlain and other "wounded committed to my care" on June 19. He did not indicate if his other patients traveled by ambulance or stretcher.

"My bearers were none too many" as they set out on that "blazing day," Chamberlain remembered. The soldiers "tried to screen my face from the burning sun" and repeatedly lay "moistened" cloths on his face. Chamberlain always regretted not getting their names.

The stretcher bearers reached the City Point wharves, and there the cool, competent Townsend blew up. Although his "life depended on the constant care of an expert," Chamberlain "did not meet that reception from the Surgeon in charge of" the hospital transport *Connecticut*, Townsend spat in ink.

He believed Chamberlain's "merits and necessities demanded" a much better response from the doctor,

"Asst. Surg. [Thomas B.] Hood," but "it was with great difficulty that I succeeded in gaining his . . . attention for a moment," Townsend noted.

Dr. Edward B. Dalton ordered Chamberlain placed on the *Connecticut*. As "Chief Medical Officer," Dalton had supervised setting up the 10,000-patient "Depot Field Hospital of the Army of the Potomac."

Carried aboard the steamer, Chamberlain went onto the main deck among hundreds of wounded suffering "for lack of proper care. We were in wretched condition;—broken, maimed, torn, stiffened with clotted blood and mattered hair and beard . . ."

And then there was Hood, who had "braced himself a little too much for his task," Chamberlain politely described the surgeon as drunk. The colonel watched Hood stagger across the stretcher-littered deck; he "came near going over backwards."

Isabella Fogg left Calais, Maine, to work as a nurse after her son left for war in 1861. (msa)

Learning that Chamberlain was on the *Connecticut*, Maine nurse Isabella Fogg climbed aboard and "volunteered to attend" him as far as the destination hospital, Townsend noted. A seamstress from Calais, she had followed her son, Hugh, and the 6th Maine to war and had cared for Maine boys on the Peninsula and after Antietam.

Joining Fogg beside Chamberlain was Joseph Linscott from Co. G, 20th Maine. Warren had ordered him to accompany Chamberlain as far as Brunswick. Townsend viewed Linscott, a hospital steward, as a qualified "nurse" and left him aboard the *Connecticut*.

The next day, Townsend learned that Hood had kicked Linscott off the ship and "in impolite language refused to allow" Fogg to stay aboard. She soon complained to Townsend about her "ungentlemanly treatment" by Hood.

Other nurses may have voiced similar complaints; Hood soon claimed the female nurses "were excluded under general instructions from the department." Women had served on hospital transports at least since the Peninsula Campaign, so he knew better.

Twice denied onboard medical care, Chamberlain lay amidst the "hardly breathing bodies." Suddenly a friend emerged from all the pain and horror aboard the steamer.

I Don't Feel Right Yet

CHAPTER SEVEN
JUNE 19 - MID-DECEMBER 1864

While caring for Union casualties on the steamer *Connecticut* late on Sunday, June 19, Dr. Thomas Freeman Moses learned that Joshua Chamberlain lay wounded on the main deck. Down a nearby ladder scrambled the good doctor, then "in charge of the upper deck."

From Bath on the Kennebec River in Maine, Moses had studied medicine at Bowdoin College ('57) and Jefferson Medical College in Philadelphia ('61). Knowing Horace Chamberlain (a classmate) and his oldest brother, Joshua (Bowdoin faculty), he found the latter on the packed main deck and stayed with him "virtually . . . all that dismal night" as the hospital transport left City Point and steamed up Chesapeake Bay.

Rated at a 400-bed capacity, the overcrowded Connecticut deposited its patients, "some sixty officers" and 465 enlisted men, "all . . . severely wounded," at Annapolis after dark on June 20, noted Reverend Henry C. Henries, a Bangor minister serving as the U.S. General Hospital chaplain.

Left unattended in a tent longer than he thought necessary, Chamberlain soon met his nurse, Mary T. Clark from Massachusetts, and his assigned surgeon, Dr. Bernard Vanderkieft, the hospital's surgeon in charge.

Did they know their patient was dying?

"Col. J. L. Chamberlain . . . was mortally wounded, it is thought . . . the ball having passed through the pelvis and bladder," Maj. Gen. Gouverneur Warren had telegraphed Maj. Gen. George Meade late on June 19.

The War Department established a major hospital at the Naval Academy at Annapolis, Maryland. (bfs)

Dr. Thomas Freeman Moses of Maine tended Joshua Chamberlain on the hospital transport *Connecticut*. (bcl)

Already "recommended for promotion [to brigadier general] for gallant and efficient conduct on previous occasions," Chamberlain had asked for promotion "before he dies for the gratification of his family and friends," Warren observed. "I beg that if possible it may be done."

Meade responded that Warren's telegram had gone to Lt. Gen. Ulysses S. Grant "with the earnest recommendation that Colonel Chamberlain's wish be gratified."

In his Special Order No. 39 issued on June 20 from City Point, Grant confirmed that "Joshua L. Chamberlain . . . for meritorious and efficient services on the field of battle, and especially for gallant conduct in leading his brigade" on June 18, "is . . . hereby . . . appointed brigadier-general of U.S. Volunteers," dating to June 18.

Lincoln must approve the promotion, but Grant evidently anticipated no problems.

* * *

Upon the recommendation of Gouverneur K. Warren, Ulysses S. Grant promoted Joshua Chamberlain to brigadier general, dating to June 18. (loc)

Apparently before Chamberlain shipped for Annapolis, a surgeon inserted a silver catheter into his urethra to help him void urine. However, prolonged catheter use caused a fistula "half an inch or more in length" to develop, and "the greater part of the urine" voided "through the fistula." Often painfully inflamed, it haunted him all his life.

Accompanied by "two of her lady friends," the five-months-pregnant Frances Chamberlain hurried to Annapolis; Henries placed her there by June 28 tending to Joshua who was "at times suffering intensely." Yet between Fanny's loving care and several surgeons monitoring his recovery, "it is not too much to say that he has every attention that it is possible to give," Henries informed the general's "numerous friends."

The patient fluctuated between life and death, believed Lt. Col. Charles D. Gilmore after visiting Chamberlain on July 3-4. "His wound is a very severe one and a very dangerous one, the surgeons are by no means certain of saving his life," Gilmore wrote Maine Adjutant Gen. John L. Hodsdon.

Gilmore explained that the minié ball had nicked Chamberlain's urethra "so near the bladder" that the surgeons could not artificially collect "all the urine" from it. Some urine leaked through the entrance wound "on the right side of the right leg, two inches below the hip joint," Gilmore wrote. "It is feared that ulcers will form in the abdomen & terminate his life."

Before leaving Bangor for Annapolis several days later, Reverend John C. Chamberlain wrote Hodsdon that Joshua "was worse," facing "a crisis . . . about this time." John Chamberlain hastened to Maryland with a Hodsdon-supplied letter opening doors en route. He reached Annapolis on Saturday, July 16 to find Joshua "in a comfortable condition," the crisis "turned favorably" toward healing.

John spent at least a week with his brother, who "has gained perceptibly every day." The wounds "have healed greatly; on the left side entirely," and "the most excruciating of his pains have ceased." Joshua's "internal difficulties . . . have so far adjusted themselves," and "the General holds his strength wonderfully, both of body and mind. He bears his sufferings with patience and calmness," John wrote.

Mustered out in mid-June 1864 after three years' service, Horatio Sickel immediately raised the 198th Pennsylvania. (loc)

With the Naval School at Annapolis now a war hospital, Reverend John S. Sewall read in the morning paper that "my old college friend" Chamberlain recovered there "from a terrible wound. The rebs at Petersburg had tried hard with shot and shell to demolish him; but he decided to live, I presume just to spite them."

Sewall scoured the Annapolis hospital for Chamberlain and "discovered him finally at the library," so well recovered that, by leaning on Fanny and Sewall, he hobbled to his tent. The comrades "had a jolly talk over old college days" and "a more sober discussion" about the never-ending war.

Chamberlain showed Sewall "the penciled scrap of paper" from Grant, announcing the battlefield promotion. "It was one hero doing honor to another hero," Sewall said.

Gilmore had brought to Chamberlain in early July his brigadier's commission, issued by Edwin Stanton, and a copy of the Senate-passed resolution confirming the promotion. "He had earned this promotion long ago," Gilmore commented. "He had been a most gallant and worthy officer[,] and . . . Maine should be proud to own him as one of her sons."

Despite his wound, "I long to be in the field again[,] doing my part to keep the old flag up, with all

Ben Butler commanded at Bermuda Hundred, to which Horatio Sickel and the 198th Pennsylvania were inexplicably diverted. (loc)

its stars," Chamberlain told Maine Governor Samuel Cony on Wednesday, August 31.

The patient had a long row to hoe, however. "My recovery is going slowly," he admitted. "I am able to sit up a good part of the day," and "time only is needed to complete any restoration to health."

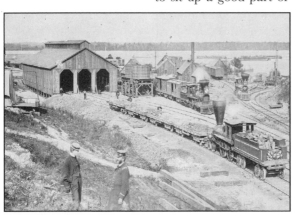

"His wounds are slowly but surely healing," reported a Maine paper. "It is said that not one in a hundred of wounds so severe as his ever terminate favorably."

As his strength returned, Chamberlain soon read in New York papers the "notices and editorials" describing "how I died. It was quite cheerful reading for a live man I can assure you!" He rejoined the war effort by recommending to Cony particular officers seeking promotion, such as Capt. Adelbert Twitchell, the 7th Maine Battery commander lobbying to become the "Major of the Light Artillery Regt. from our state." "Well acquainted" with Twitchell, Chamberlain described him as "a true man," possessing a "high character which he ... so nobly maintains."

The U.S. Military Railroad transported the 198th Pennsylvania from City Point to V Corps at Petersburg. (na)

Although an often-cited postwar source claimed that Chamberlain "was furloughed September 20, 1864," his September 22 letter to Cony placed the general at "Officer's Hospital, Annapolis" on that date. Fanny brought him home later that month to recover.

*   *   *

William Tilton commanded the 1st Brigade during the August 18-21 battle of the Weldon Railroad. (loc)

Chamberlain would not stay away from the war. Aware that "these terrible wounds . . . must cast a shadow over the remainder of my days," he admitted to his mother, Sarah, that "what it is, I cannot tell you" that drove him Virginia-ward.

"I haven't a particle of fanaticism in me," yet "I plead guilty to a sort of fatalism," he wrote. 'I believe in a destiny—one, I mean, divinely appointed, and to which we are carried forward by a perfect trust in God."

For Chamberlain, that destiny meant rejoining the army. Unable to mount a horse unaided or walk very far, he reported to V Corps headquarters on November 19. He resumed 1st Brigade command that day.

He had missed the August 18-21 battle of the Weldon Railroad, during which the 1st Brigade (led by Col. William S. Tilton) suffered 71 casualties, including 46 men "captured or missing." The army soon reconfigured the brigade by replacing the six Pennsylvania infantry regiments with the 21st Pennsylvania Cavalry (Dismounted) and the 198th Pennsylvania Infantry, a Union League outfit recruited at Harrisburg in midsummer. Its command went to Col. Horatio G. Sickel, a Bucks County native who had served for three years until mustering out in mid-June 1864.

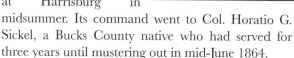

An embrasure frames a cannon at these recreated earthworks at Petersburg National Battlefield. (bfs)

Sickel lent his name and reputation to raising the 198th, mustered on September 15 and shipped by train to Baltimore. Bumping into Ulysses S. Grant there, Sickel requested assignment with the Army of the Potomac. Granted his wish, he saw his regiment briefly diverted by red tape to Ben Butler at Bermuda Hundred before being sent to City Point late on June 25. The Pennsylvanians reached the docks the next morning, a quartermaster refused them passage on the only available steamer, and Sickel promptly threatened to "seize her in the name of General Grant."

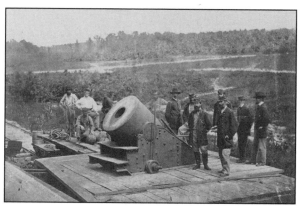

Union gunners man the massive, railroad-transported mortar called "The Dictator." (loc)

Union infantry tear up tracks and burn buildings at Jarratt's Station on the Weldon Railroad on December 8, 1864.
(loc)

After returning from the Weldon Railroad raid, Joshua Chamberlain shared the details in a letter to his sister, Sarah Brastow Chamberlain.
(phcc)

The quartermaster backed down, and the 198th arrived off City Point a few hours later. Transported by the U.S. Military Railroad to "the extreme left" flank, the Pennsylvanians reported to Warren. Charles Griffin then marched the 198th "to the First Brigade headquarters" and gave Sickel brigade command, "General Chamberlain being absent, wounded."

Larger than a typical infantry regiment, the 198th was "a regiment of two batallions of seven companies each," so Sickel led a relatively large brigade during the battle of Peebles' Farm (also called "Poplar Spring Church" and "Pegram's Farm"), fought September 30-October 2. The brigade suffered 21 casualties.

Early on October 27, Warren maneuvered V Corps to support an advance against the Southside Railroad. New regiments fleshed out Griffin's 1st Division; although "4707 strong," its ranks included 1,247 soldiers "ignorant of the [drill] manual" and 2,803 men who "had never fired a musket."

In October the army again reorganized Griffin's 1st Brigade, replacing the 21st Pennsylvania Cavalry with the 185th New York, commanded by Col. Gustavus Sniper. Recruited in Cortland and Onondaga counties in upstate New York in late August, the 185th New York had mustered on September 22-23. Shipped directly to City Point, the regiment received "no opportunity for preliminary drill or discipline" and "was . . . placed on active service" in the Petersburg lines.

The 185th New York joined the 198th Pennsylvania in Sickel's 1st Brigade. The late October Union advance against Robert E. Lee's right flank resulted in the battle of Boydton Plank Road (also called First Hatcher's Run or Burgess Farm). The 1st Brigade lost eight men.

Chamberlain took over the 1st Brigade on November 19. Sickel rejoined the 198th. The brigade moved out with V Corps early on December 7 to raid the Weldon Railroad. Warren took along a cavalry division, three divisions from V Corps, a II Corps division, four artillery batteries, and a 250-foot "canvas pontoon bridge."

A cold rain encumbered the march to the Nottoway River, reached by V Corps' advance elements around dark. Crossing on the pontoon bridge before dawn on December 8, Union troops worked south, destroying the railroad well into the night. Plagued by rain and flooding streams, the expedition tore up the Weldon Railroad as far as Belfield on the Meherrin River's north bank, across from Confederate-fortified Hicksford.

Writing to his sister Sarah, Chamberlain described how the Union soldiers took up the railroad tracks and shook apart the steel rails from the wood ties. Stacking the latter "up to a sharp ridge," the soldiers placed the rails atop the pile, leaving the rails "balanced so that the weight of the ends will bend the rail nearly double when heated.

"Then set fire [to the ties], & you see a grand sight," Chamberlain wrote. "The next morning you see a ruin," primarily "the bent & useless rails. Well, we left 20 miles in that shape."

As Warren returned to Petersburg, "the enemy's scouts & guerrillas" captured and "murdered" some Union stragglers, found with "their throats cut from ear to ear," Chamberlain wrote.

Wood huts like this replica at Petersburg National Battlefield served as winter quarters for Union soldiers. (bfs)

"Angry Union soldiers burnt almost every house on the road," despite his "sad work in protecting helpless women & children from outrage" while commanding the rear guard "one day," Chamberlain wrote. Although guerrillas fired from some houses, he set guards to protect women and their homes, "but I have no doubt they were all 'burnt out' before the whole army got by."

"I am willing to fight men in arms, but not babes in arms," he growled.

Conducted amidst cold temperatures and bone-chilling rain, "from the effects of which many of the men have never recovered," the raid had left Chamberlain aware "I 'was not fit' to return to field duty.

"I ride some, too much, probably & to tell the truth, I don't feel right yet," he admitted. "I shall have to take to the knife" for surgery to repair his wound.

He finally sought help outside the army.

Hell for Ten Minutes and We Are Out of It!

CHAPTER EIGHT

MID-JANUARY - MARCH 29, 1865

In mid-January 1865, Joshua Chamberlain sought surgical repair from Dr. Joseph Pancoast, the Department of Anatomy chairman and a professor of surgery at Jefferson Medical College in Philadelphia. Renowned by mid-century for developing improved surgical procedures, he had published *A Treatise on Operative Surgery* in 1844.

His surgery on Chamberlain involved "stricture dilation" (also known as urethral dilation), designed "to stretch the scar tissue without injuring the lining of the urethra." The patient survived the painful procedure, and late January found him in Brunswick, "confined to his house, suffering much from his wound,—a very severe one and healing slowly."

Chamberlain arrived home to a warm reception from his children Wyllys and Grace and from Fanny, who introduced her husband to Gertrude Loraine Chamberlain, born on January 16. Would not the battered warrior settle into domesticity? He certainly had sacrificed enough to save the Union.

"Surely, you have done & suffered & won laurels enough in this war to satisfy the most ambitious," Sarah Chamberlain wrote her eldest son on January 1. Hopefully he was "moved by nobler motives" rather "than the praise of man alone" to seek additional military glory.

Despite the sleigh-riding, skating, and other wintry recreation romantically depicted in mid-nineteenth

Gravelly Run flows quietly where the Quaker Road crosses the stream in Dinwiddie County, Virginia. (loc)

A renowned surgeon, Dr. Joseph Pancoast was the professor of anatomy at Jefferson Medical College. (loc)

While home recovering from his wound in winter 1865, Joshua Chamberlain and his parents disputed by letter his plans to rejoin the army. (msa)

century lithographs, snow-covered roads limited travel in a Maine winter. Rather than let his body recover as he relaxed by the fireside and enjoyed family life, the battered warrior chafed at his inaction.

"Still confined mostly to my room," Chamberlain responded after his father urged him in early February to take a political appointment as Collector of Customs at Bath, 10 miles east of Brunswick. The federal position offered a steady income, required little strenuous physical exertion, and kept the appointee far from the war.

While tempted—he had spent "the past week" debating the admittedly "very good position"—Chamberlain preferred "to continue my duties in the field, where my services were never more needed, or more valuable than now." With army life "most congenial to my temperament," he sought involvement in an "enterprise of a more bold & stirring character than a College chair affords."

His parents apparently reiterated their support for the Customs position. "I appreciate fully the view you & Mother take" on the subject, Chamberlain wrote his father on February 20, but "I owe the Country three years service.

"It is a time when every man should stand by his guns," he explained. "And I am not scared or hurt enough yet to be willing to face to the rear, when other men are marching to the front."

He may have alluded to news arriving from army comrades and also articles appearing in the Brunswick and Portland newspapers. On February 5, V Corps had pushed southwest into Dinwiddie County and, along with two divisions from II Corps and a cavalry division, had fought the three-day battle of Hatcher's Run. The 1st Brigade he left in mid-January was there, but Chamberlain was not.

Acknowledging "my incomplete recovery from my wounds" and his importance to "my young & dependent family," Chamberlain heard the guns sounding more loudly than protests raised by wife and parents.

"I am now among the Senior officers of my rank," and with the Army of the Potomac poised to clobber Robert E. Lee that spring, Chamberlain "would rather see another man in that Custom House, than see another next commander of the 1st Division."

He "would not abandon our cause in the hour of its need," and "I must return to the army," he wrote. "I shall leave tomorrow." Chamberlain boarded a southbound train at Brunswick on Tuesday, February 21. His wound flared along the way; "detained in Philadelphia" by his medical issues, he sought help from Pancoast, "the most skilful surgeon in the United States." His ministrations "not only relieved my existing disabilities, but put me in the mood of a more rapid recovery," Chamberlain told his sister, Sarah.

Returning to the two-regiment 1st Brigade, Chamberlain shed the ennui affecting him at home. "You cannot imagine how favorable this kind of life is to my health," he wrote. In Brunswick, he might "walk a half mile," yet "here I ride as fast & far as the best, and ask no favors."

While hoping for "a speedy return to the happiness and affection of my little home," Chamberlain claimed "the dangers . . . threatening me threaten them tenfold." Fulfilling his duty, "which honor and manliness prompt," would "prove best for them & for all who belong to me or to whom I belong."

He returned to an Army of the Potomac still recognizable from mid-January. Gouverneur K. Warren commanded V Corps, Charles Griffin led the 1st Division, and Horatio Sickel its 1st Brigade. Familiar faces welcomed Chamberlain back.

By winter 1865, Robert E. Lee had extended the Confederacy's siege lines well west of Petersburg. These Confederate earthworks are located at Pamplin Park. (bfs)

* * *

Then Maj. Gen. Phil Sheridan arrived on March 27. The hyperkinetic warrior had torn apart Jubal Early's army in the Shenandoah Valley. Ulysses S. Grant expected similar success by Sheridan against the ill-clad, gaunt Confederates defending Richmond and Petersburg.

Confederates held a 37-mile line running from White Oak Swamp "on their left, to the Clairborne-road crossing of Hatcher's Run, on their right," with "sixteen [miles] on the Petersburg line," noted Maj. Gen. Andrew Humphreys, the II Corps commander.

Grant planned to push farther west until Union troops could turn the Confederates' right flank and cut the Southside Railroad. On March 24, he issued the order that launched the flanking movement five days later.

But out of March 25's pre-dawn darkness streamed thousands of Confederates to capture Fort Stedman, puncture the Union siege lines, and roll up the Federal defenders as far as the Appomattox River. The fort and some adjacent batteries fell, and Maj. Gen. John B. Gordon's men pushed farther before arriving Union infantry sealed the hole and, aided by fast-firing artillery in the forts on either side of Stedman, shattered the enemy attack.

Warren had already turned out V Corps to help. "At early dawn" Chamberlain and the 1st Brigade "hurriedly got under arms, and double-quicked . . . some two miles to re-enforce" the IX Corps, recalled E. Morrison Woodward of the 198th Pennsylvania.

The brigade bounced around behind II and VI corps, "whenever their support seemed most urgent," and often came under enemy fire although "not actually engaged," Woodward said. The maneuvering continued all day, and the "completely worn out" Pennsylvanians reached their camp in late evening.

Suffering from malnutrition and inadequate clothing, Confederate troops lived in log huts and rude shelters such as this example at Pamplin Park. (bfs)

At 3:00 a.m., Wednesday, March 29, Warren and V Corps opened the final campaign against the Army of Northern Virginia. Night hung heavy as Maj. Gen. Romeyn B. Ayres and his vanguard 2nd Division headed south for where the Stage Road crossed Rowanty Creek, the larger stream formed by the intersecting Gravelly Run and Hatcher's Run. Ayres marched with "about 3,980 men," Warren noted.

The 3rd Division (Maj. Gen. Samuel W. Crawford) marched "5,260 strong" behind Ayres and two artillery batteries. Bringing up the rear, from his

1st Division camps near where the Vaughan Road crossed Hatcher's Run, Maj. Gen. Charles Griffin brought out 6,547 men in three brigades: the 1st (Brig. Gen. Joshua L. Chamberlain), the 2nd (Brig. Gen. Edgar M. Gregory), and the 3rd (Brig. Gen. Joseph J. Bartlett).

For a while Fort Wadsworth was the westernmost post in the Union siege lines. (bfs)

The day dawned warm, and the air stirred by a southerly "moist wind." Swinging out at 6 a.m., Chamberlain and his brigade cut south by east across "Arthur's Swamp" (also Arthur's Creek or Arthur's Run) to turn west on "the old stage road."

Ayres's lead brigade reached the Rowanty at 4:45 a.m. Southern pickets fired "a few shots" before scattering, and "the engineers speedily laid a canvas pontoon bridge" while infantry crossed "on fallen trees" and a ruined bridge (known as Monk's Neck Bridge), Warren reported. Once over the stream, his men removed the felled trees blocking the Monk's Neck Road, and his vanguard reached the Vaughan Road intersection "at 8 a.m."

The V Corps advanced into Dinwiddie County while relying on an ancient map just "republished for our use at a scale of one inch to the mile," Warren said. He marched almost blind. The map indicated only "the main streams and main roads," differentiated not between "the forest and clearings or swamps," and identified houses by their owners' surnames. Some houses had new owners, other houses had vanished, and newer houses were unmarked on the map.

The V Corps turned out when John Gordon launched an initially successful March 25 attack against Fort Stedman. (bfs)

Phil Sheridan swiftly launched an end run around Confederate defenses outside Petersburg after reaching the Army of the Potomac on March 27, 1865. (na)

Heavily forested, the "level" Dinwiddie terrain was "well watered by swampy streams," Warren said, and clay or sand formed the soil, which "where these mix together, [was] like quicksand." Once the winter frost melted, "the soil is very light and soft, and hoofs and wheels find but little support," he observed.

Similar to the rural roads Chamberlain knew while growing up in Brewer, country roads meandered everywhere in Dinwiddie County. Where a teenage Chamberlain could ride out from Brewer to Clewleyville Corner in Holden and, depending onto which road he turned, get lost among the woods, hills, farms, and fields, the 36-year-old warrior could wind up God knew where by venturing onto any Dinwiddie road. He would tour several such roads today with the 1st Brigade, momentarily numbering "1750 men for duty," some "450 short of its normal numbers." Gustavus Sniper led the 185th New York and Horatio G. Sickel the 14-company 198th Pennsylvania.

The 1st Division's vanguard, Chamberlain's brigade reached the Oliver Chappell house about two miles east of Dinwiddie Courthouse sometime before noon. The brigade might have rested a while had not Meade fretted about Maj. Gen. Andrew Humphreys and II Corps.

After V Corps had marched south that morning, II Corps had "crossed Hatcher's Run at the Vaughan road . . . and moved in an extended line [west], over

Growing up in Brewer, Joshua Chamberlain possibly explored the Clewleyville Road intersection not far from home; from here he would have wandered into remote places like those found in rural Dinwiddie County. (bfs)

a densely wooded and difficult country" some four miles northeast of V Corps, wrote Maj. E. Morrison Woodward, the 198th Pennsylvania's historian. This placed Humphreys much nearer than V Corps to the enemy's westernmost Petersburg defenses, extending along the White Oak Road to turn about a mile north on the Claiborne Road.

Part of Lt. Gen. Richard H. Anderson's corps, Confederate Maj. Gen. Bushrod R. Johnson and his division held that section. His four brigade commanders were Brig. Gen. Henry A. Wise (four Virginia regiments); Brig. Gen. William Henry Wallace (five South Carolina regiments and Holcombe's South Carolina Legion); Brig. Gen. Young M. Moody (four Alabama regiments and the 23rd Alabama Battalion); and Brig. Gen. Matthew W. Ransom (five North Carolina regiments). Four artillery battalions rounded out Fourth Corps.

Worried the enemy would strike Humphreys, by mid-morning Meade ordered Warren to push north on the Quaker Road to find the Southern positions. As directed by Griffin, Chamberlain marched his brigade up the Vaughan Road, swung left onto the Quaker Road, and probed "in a northerly direction" to Gravelly Run.

Confederates had destroyed the bridge and built "some defenses on the north bank," which rises above the stream. With Griffin's permission, Chamberlain deployed Sickel and eight of the 198th's companies "on the right," downstream (east) from the bridge, and took the other six companies and the 185th New York "above the bridge" (west). Griffin brought up the 2nd

Andrew Humphreys had served as Meade's chief of staff since shortly after the Gettysburg campaign, but he had amassed a solid service record prior to that and chaffed to go back to field command. Meade granted his wish in November 1864 when Winfield Scott Hancock stepped down from command of the II Corps. (loc)

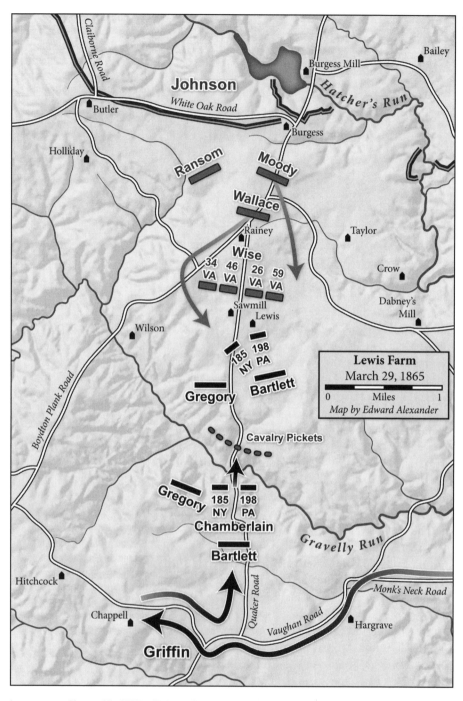

LEWIS FARM, MARCH 29, 1865—Detoured to support II Corps, Joshua Chamberlain and the 1st Brigade probed north along the Quaker Road until encountering Confederate cavalry pickets loosely holding Gravelly Run's far bank. Dislodging the pickets, the brigadier and his men advanced north and struck Confederate troops at the Lewis farm.

Brigade on Chamberlain's left and positioned the 3rd Brigade in support behind Chamberlain.

When Sickel's men suddenly poured "a hot fire upon the enemy opposite," Maj. Edwin A. Glenn waded Gravelly Run with the remaining 198th companies and attacked the Confederate defenders "front and flank," Chamberlain recalled. Across the stream went Sickel, Sniper, and their men, "and the whole command swept onward like a wave . . . for a mile or more" to the Lewis farm.

Past Gravelly Run, the Quaker Road curved uphill, then straightened beyond the crest and pointed almost due north to the Boydton Plank Road. Wide farm fields stretched to distant tree lines around the Lewis farm, past which Glenn and his Pennsylvanians drove the retreating enemy.

Anderson had ordered Johnson to attack the Union troops coming north. Wise shook out a "line of battle" and probed south on the Quaker Road, but Confederate cavalry reported the Yankees "retiring beyond Gravelly Run," Johnson said. "I therefore did not expect to encounter them" until reaching the stream, he commented.

Johnson's three remaining brigades followed Wise. Reaching the tree lines north of the Lewis farm, his men traded fire with Glenn, then charged "at 3.20 p.m.," Wise reported.

"The enemy making considerable show of force" along the tree lines north of the farm buildings, Chamberlain halted Glenn and brought up the brigade's line of battle. Studying the terrain, Griffin ordered an attack. Reinforcing Glenn with a 185th New York company, Chamberlain took his men forward.

Woodward described the "clear field" as "one thousand yards deep and wide," with "heavy timber" on either side. Confederate sharpshooters nestled like gray squirrels in the hardwoods and pines. Ahead, along the tree line, lay "a substantial breastwork of logs and earth," and nearer Quaker Road "a heap of sawdust where a portable mill had stood," said Chamberlain. Woodward described the structure as "an old saw mill," and a 185th New York survivor recalled "the saw-dust pile." Men had little time to study it before "a withering volley" tore apart Chamberlain's skirmishers and battle line.

Carrying their wounded and dead, his men started backwards, moving slowly. Boiling from their earthworks, Confederates ordered forward by Wise plowed into the Union boys; fighting quickly disintegrated to "hand in hand in eddying currents," Chamberlain recalled.

The rising southerly wind blew gunsmoke into Confederate faces, throwing off Southern accuracy, and Chamberlain's lads grabbed a hundred prisoners. A Union charge cleared the field, and the 1st Brigade pulled back to the farm buildings, reformed, and waited.

Describing Wise's men as "driven back from the woods to the open ground," Johnson deployed Wallace to support Wise. Moody soon moved his brigade in support into the woods on Wise's left.

Horatio Sickel and eight companies of the 198th Pennsylvania waded Gravelly Run from right to left at approximately this point. (bfs)

"We had been repulsed," Chamberlain admitted, and that would not do, Griffin decided. Placing Sickel and the 198th on the right and Sniper and the 185th on the left, "I took Major Glenn and his six companies for a straight dash up the Quaker Road," Chamberlain said.

His men moving "at the double quick," he targeted the earthworks at the piled sawdust. Gunsmoke puffed from the trees as the enemy sharpshooters fired; Yankees fell, a few fired despite orders not to do so, and the excitable Charlemagne ran faster "than the men."

Chamberlain hauled hard on the reins. Charlemagne reared "head-high to the level of my face" just before a bullet punched through the horse's "big [neck] muscle" and struck Chamberlain in the left breast-pocket, "just below the heart." He collapsed unconscious "on my horse's neck."

The bullet struck and "bruised and battered" his raised "bridle (left) arm" before puncturing a brass-rimmed hand mirror and paperwork-stuffed leather case in the pocket, deflecting "around two ribs," and exiting "at the back seam of my coat," Chamberlain

Chamberlain and his 1st Brigade advanced about a mile north on the Quaker Road before slamming into Southern troops at the Lewis farm. (bfs)

recalled. The bullet then "demolished" an aide's belt-mounted pistol "and knocked him out of the saddle."

Charlemagne stood still as Griffin rode up, placed an arm around Chamberlain's waist, and quietly said, "My dear General, you are gone."

Hearing "a wild rebel yell" to the right (east), Chamberlain raised his head and saw his right flank "broken and flying before the enemy." Responding to Griffin, "Yes, General, I am," he turned his horse (now "bleeding profusely") to the right, and rode to rally his men.

"I must have been a queer spectacle as I rode in the saddle tattered and battered, bare-headed and blood-smeared," Chamberlain thought. Riding among the retreating Pennsylvanians, he found "the brave Sickel, his face aflame, rallying his men." Regrouping, the 198th "straightened up into line" and drove back Wise's Virginians. His left arm severely wounded, Sickel fell; his war was over.

As Chamberlain rode "back to the center," Charlemagne slowed and stopped. His rider dismounted and went afoot until brought a "strange, dull-looking white horse" splotched with red mud.

Noticing Wise's retreating Virginians, Richard Anderson ordered Johnson to put in Wallace's South Carolinians. Johnson also brought up Moody's Alabamians, but Wallace struck the 185th New York before Moody arrived.

"Badly cut up," the New Yorkers pulled back almost parallel with the Quaker Road. Chamberlain found Sniper holding "his regimental colors" and "still holding his shattered ranks facing the enemy" after losing two color-bearers wounded, a color sergeant killed, and the color-company captain badly wounded.

Griffin arrived, promised that "if you can hold on there ten minutes, I will give you a battery," and spurred south.

Chamberlain pushed his horse through "my fine New Yorkers" to Sniper and yelled, "Once more! Try the steel! Hell for ten minutes and we are out of it!"

"A final charge was made," a New Yorker remembered, and Chamberlain rode along as the 185th advanced. He frequently looked south along the Quaker Road; suddenly he saw Battery B, 4th U.S. Artillery (1st Lt. John Mitchell) coming up, "horses smoking, battery thundering with jolt and rattle."

Chamberlain directed Mitchell onto a "knoll," and his polished bronze Napoleons swung around. "Shouts changing into shrieks" disclosed the efficacy as "the bellowing, leaping big guns" delivered air bursts among the trees surrounding the Confederates. New Yorkers fought desperately, the artillery spewed canister to shatter a final attack on the left, but "the enemy fell heavily upon our right and center,"

Confederate infantry reaching the Lewis farm tree lines charged Chamberlain's advancing brigade and briefly pushed it back. (bfs)

Confederates retreating from the Lewis farm abandoned the Quaker Road-Boydton Plank Road intersection, occupied in late afternoon by V Corps. (bfs)

sending Chamberlain's line "falling back in front of the Lewis house."

Griffin brought up the 1st and 16th Michigan and 189th Pennsylvania to support Sniper. Up came "that handsome Zouave regiment, the 155th Pennsylvania," which Chamberlain set next to Glenn in "the center."

The reinforcements went forward. Richard Anderson "now directed my division to be withdrawn, at about 5 p.m.," Bushrod Johnson said. "Our losses were about 250 men."

"It is soon over," at a price of "more than 400 of my men and 18 officers killed and wounded," Chamberlain reported. Joseph Bartlett pushed his 3rd Brigade north toward the Boydton Plank Road-White Oak Road intersection, and Johnson withdrew his Confederates into the main earthworks along the latter road later that day.

Rain started falling that evening.

Useless Sacrifice at White Oak Road

CHAPTER NINE

MARCH 29 - 31, 1865

Dinwiddie County overflowed as rain poured from Virginia's skies overnight on March 29 and throughout Thursday, March 30. Aching from his latest wound, Brig. Gen. Joshua L. Chamberlain remembered "the chilling rain . . . soaking the fields and roads and drenching the men stretched on the ground, worn, wounded, and dying" alike on that "dark and dismal night."

"Before morning the roads were impassable for wagons or artillery," he realized.

Horace Porter, an aide to Ulysses S. Grant, recalled how "whole fields" became "beds of quicksand" into which horses and wagons sank deeply. The roads disintegrated into such "sheets of water"—veritable streams—that a soldier shouted at the passing Porter, "I say, when are the gun-boats coming up?"

Despite "the sodden earth and miry roads," V Corps pushed west Thursday morning, beyond "the Boydton Plank Road . . . as far as its crossing of Gravelly Run," Chamberlain reported.

His battered 1st Brigade went into reserve as Maj. Gen. Charles Griffin advanced the 2nd Brigade (Brig. Gen. Edgar M. Gregory) and the 3rd Brigade (Brig. Gen. Joseph J. Bartlett) into the rifle pits abandoned Wednesday by Confederates retreating to their White Oak Road entrenchments. Griffin shook out a picket line "within easy range of the enemy's main works."

Weathered earthworks define a Southern artillery emplacement alongside White Oak Road, at a point near Robert E. Lee's far right flank. (bfs)

Wartime aide Horace Porter served as personal secretary to President Ulysses S. Grant.
(loc)

"The rain fell incessantly during the day and but little was done," he said.

His right flank afloat, a nervous Maj. Gen. Gouverneur K. Warren swapped messages throughout the morning with Griffin, Maj. Gen. Andrew Humphreys of II Corps, and Maj. Gen. Andrew S. Webb, chief of staff to Lt. Gen. Ulysses S. Grant. Warren dared not probe north toward White Oak Road without II Corps positioned on his right flank, but Grant wanted the V Corps, its left flank already anchored on Gravelly Run, to "extend to the left as far as possible."

So Warren shifted Maj. Gen. Romeyn B. Ayres and his 2nd Division to V Corps' far left flank, with an eye to pushing southwest toward Dinwiddie Courthouse, occupied by Maj. Gen. Philip Sheridan and his cavalry.

What if Warren also brought over Maj. Gen. Sam Crawford and his 3rd Division to help Ayres? "If the enemy turns my left, what will I have to attack him with?" Warren asked Webb.

But Humphreys was already supporting Warren. Brigadier General Nelson A. Miles started his 1st Division of II Corps moving west at 6:00 a.m. "through an almost impassable country" to the Dabney Mill Road. By midafternoon, Miles's left flank abutted the Boydton Plank Road and touched Warren's right flank.

Miles sent his 2nd Brigade to corduroy the Dabney Mill Road, "in a very bad condition" due "to the heavy rain," and ordered "temporary works . . . thrown up . . . and bivouacked for the night." Behind Miles moved Brig. Gen. Gershom Mott and his 3rd Division, II Corps.

After meeting with Sheridan at army headquarters Thursday morning, Grant told Maj. Gen. George G. Meade that the army should extend its left flank across White Oak Road, perhaps as far as "Ford's road" at Five Forks. Sheridan could hurl his cavalry up the latter road to interdict the Southside Railroad.

Warren read his copy of the dispatch at noon and then rode "up the Quaker Road" to examine what lay in front of Griffin. Joining the 1st Division skirmishers as they pushed back their Southern counterparts, he examined the stout Confederate earthworks, "defended by infantry and artillery."

To protect the Southside Railroad, on March 28 Robert E. Lee had ordered Maj. Gen. Fitzhugh Lee and his cavalry division to start on the long trot "from the extreme left of our lines" at Richmond south to Petersburg, then 19 miles west to Sutherland Station on March 29, the cavalry commander recalled.

During Thursday's deluge, he probed "toward Dinwiddie Court-House, via Five Forks," drove off Union cavalry, and camped near Five Forks. That evening major generals William H. F. "Rooney" Lee and Thomas L. Rosser and their cavalry divisions joined Fitzhugh Lee, now commanding "the Cavalry Corps" and its 3,200 to 4,000 troopers (depending on Rooney Lee's changeable nose count).

Despite his wartime exploits, Nelson Miles garnered greater fame during the Indian wars of the 1870s and '80s. (loc)

Robert E. Lee also shifted Maj. Gen. George E. Pickett and his division to Five Forks. After Pickett arrived on March 30, Lee swapped infantry brigades. From behind the Claiborne-White Oak road earthworks, Bushrod Johnson detached Matthew W. Ransom and William Henry Wallace and their brigades for duty with Pickett, who sent Brig. Gen. Eppa Hunton and his all-Virginia brigade "for duty with my command," Johnson said.

Early Friday morning found the V Corps amidst the Gravelly Run headwaters, northwest of the Boydton Plank Road. In front, Ayres and his 2nd Division deployed within 600 yards of Johnson's defenses at the Claiborne-White Oak road intersection. Crawford and his 3rd Division were in echelon some 600 yards to Ayres' right and rear.

Some 1,300 yards behind Crawford's left flank, the 1st Division spread "along the southeast bank of a swampy" Gravelly Run tributary, Chamberlain said. Facing north toward the 2nd Division, his brigade held "the extreme left of our lines," while Gregory's 2nd Brigade formed a "refused" line facing west on "a country road" running north from the Boydton Plank Road to the Claiborne Road.

With artillery batteries now bolstering his defenses, the rain stopping, and the day dawning cloudy, Chamberlain nervously eyed the stream-laced terrain to the west. Prisoners taken elsewhere revealed that George Pickett prowled just beyond "the exposed left flank of the Fifth and Second Corps."

Robert E. Lee pulled cavalry and infantry from elsewhere along the Petersburg lines to counter the Union maneuver against his right flank. (loc)

To the east, Nelson Miles of the II Corps had spread his division across the Boydton Plank-Quaker road intersection somewhere on Griffin's right flank. Fortunately for Chamberlain, Pickett went elsewhere during Friday's daylight.

* * *

Senior Union commanders believed the sodden terrain barred offensive operations on March 31. Meade ordered Warren to hold in place "owing to the weather." Fifth Corps' supply wagons struggled eastward to load ammunition, rations, and forage at the westernmost U.S. Military Railroad station.

The morning passed quietly until around 9:45 a.m., when Warren, responding to a Romeyn Ayres report, ordered him to push back the enemy pickets south of White Oak Road. They came from the 41st Alabama (Col. Martin L. Stansel), part of Brig. Gen. Young M. Moody's brigade.

Reading the instructions to Ayres, at 10:30 a.m. Meade ordered Warren to "get possession of and hold the White Oak road," depending on what Ayres's "reconnaissance" turned up.

Warren's order, delivered by Maj. E. B. Cope, instructed Ayres to interdict and defend White Oak Road. Ayres moved north with Brig. Gen. Frederick Winthrop and his all-New York 1st Brigade leading "in line of battle," followed at the "right and rear" by Brig. Gen. James Gwyn and his 3rd Brigade, Chamberlain later reported.

"Formed in column on Winthrop's left and rear" was the "Maryland Brigade" of Brig. Gen. Andrew W. Denison, Chamberlain noted. Sam Crawford, the 3rd Division's commander, placed a brigade "in reserve in rear of the center." The 2nd Division advanced "in a wedge-like formation guarding both flanks," Chamberlain said.

Stansel's Alabamians reported the approaching enemy by 11:00 a.m., and Bushrod Johnson decided to attack. Forming a line of battle, he put Brig. Gen. Samuel McGowan and his South Carolina brigade on the right, Moody's brigade (commanded by Stansel) in the center, and Hunton's brigade on the left. "I immediately ordered my command to . . . meet the enemy's attack," Johnson said.

Only 50 yards separated Winthrop and his New Yorkers from White Oak Road when Johnson's infantry "rose up in the woods and moved forward across the road into the open," Ayres said. He estimated the Confederates "had four or five [soldiers] to my one." "The enemy's onset was swift and the encounter sudden," Chamberlain learned. Emerging from concealing woods, McGowan "struck squarely on Winthrop's left flank," while Moody and Hunton hit "his front and right."

Ayres watched Winthrop's brigade turn around and march south "in good order." Then the New Yorkers broke, Denison went down wounded amidst his brigade, and the 2nd Division collapsed, pouring panicked soldiers through the 3rd Division's ranks.

Commanding the latter division's 1st Brigade, Col. John A. Kellogg attempted to stop the refugees "flying in confusion from the field," but could not do so with "the men breaking through my line and throwing my own command into confusion." Sam Crawford pulled back his brigades; Kellogg came away "shooting rapidly" to both flanks and his rear, Confederates so close that his men had "to fight their way back."

Charles Griffin brought Bartlett's brigade to the Gravelly Run tributary's south bank just minutes, at best, before "the Third Division [came] running to the rear in a most demoralized and disorganized condition, soon after followed by the Second Division."

"The whole crowd" thrashed across the stream and plowed into the 1st Division's right flank, Chamberlain said. Charles Griffin and Joe Bartlett drove the refugees into line behind the 3rd Brigade, which hit the pursuing Confederates with "a sharp fire of musketry and artillery."

Johnson reported driving the Yankees one and a half miles before being stopped by lead and iron. By now Robert E. Lee had ordered out Brig. Gen. Henry A. Wise and his brigade on Hunton's left. Wise might have turned V Corps' right flank, but Nelson Miles and his division thrust northwest and broke that attack.

Griffin and Warren suddenly "came down at full speed" into the 1st Brigade's lines. Ashamed that his command had broken, Warren blurted, "General Chamberlain, will you save the honor of Fifth Corps? That's all there is about it."

Officially commander of the Army of the Potomac, George Meade discovered that Ulysses S. Grant placed greater value on Phil Sheridan, nominally Meade's subordinate. (loc)

A West Point graduate, Confederate cavalry leader Fitzhugh Lee rejoined the U.S. Army during the Spanish-American War and became a major general of volunteers. (loc)

Understanding that Warren wanted him to counterattack, Chamberlain thought, "Honor is a mighty sentiment, and the Fifth Corps was dear to me," yet "my little brigade" was shot to pieces. He asked about the 3rd, "our largest and best brigade," but only his would do.

"We have come to you; you know what that means," someone replied.

Warren offered a pontoon bridge to span the tributary; "my men will go straight through," replied Chamberlain. Major Edwin A. Glenn and the 198th Pennsylvania waded "the muddy branch, waist deep," and Chamberlain crossed with his brigade and the 2nd Brigade, now seconded to him.

Chamberlain reported that the Confederates made "stand after stand" on "broken strong ground" as the Yankees pushed north. Bartlett came up in reserve, the reformed 2nd Division "on our left rear," and "Crawford . . . somewhere to our right and rear, but out of sight or reach," Chamberlain recalled.

"Our troops being exhausted" with no reinforcements available, Johnson pulled back his brigades, which briefly went into abandoned Union rifle pits south of White Oak Road. Wise reoccupied the earthworks held earlier by his brigade.

Warren ordered Chamberlain to halt on an "open field" within visual range of Southern defenses. The position was untenable, so he proposed an attack: 1st Brigade crossing the field and 2nd Brigade advancing through woods on the right. Warren approved.

"Had I known . . . that General Lee himself was personally directing affairs in our front, I might not have . . . thought myself so cool," Chamberlain admitted later.

Buglers blew "forward, and that way we go," he said. Its ranks opened up "to lessen the loss from the long-range rifles," and the 1st Brigade charged. Gustavus Sniper and the 185th New York swarmed over the defenses on the left, the 198th Pennsylvania those on the right, and Gregory and his brigade dealt with the enemy beyond Chamberlain's right flank.

Chamberlain reported the drive's success. "The seething wave of countercurrents" left "a fringe of wrecks" as the Yankees "advanced some 300 yards across" White Oak Road and drove the

Confederates into the Claiborne Road earthworks, said Chamberlain. Now facing northeast, his men started building earthworks. He pegged his losses "at not more than seventy-five."

* * *

Dismounting at 1st Brigade headquarters, Chamberlain and his aides stood quietly "on a little eminence" while "wrapped in thoughts of the declining day." He had not loosened his saddle girth when gunfire—"these heavy waves of sound"— emanated from the southwest. That should have been Phil Sheridan coming up, as expected all afternoon, on V Corps' flank to help secure the White Oak Road and turn Robert E. Lee's right flank.

His affiliation with Gettysburg overshadowed the shocking decision by George Pickett to hang 22 Union soldiers from North Carolina after the February 1864 attack on New Bern. (loc)

But Sheridan had failed to appear. Via his chief of staff, Maj. Gen. Alexander S. Webb, Ulysses S. Grant had informed Maj. Gen. Gouverneur K. Warren at 5:00 p.m. that "it is believed that Sheridan is pushing up" from Dinwiddie Courthouse. Perhaps V Corps could "push a small force down the White Oak road and try to communicate with Sheridan," but do not mistake his men for Confederates and open fire, Webb passed the word.

The visibly anxious Warren joined Chamberlain. They speculated about the gunfire, "whether it was nearing or receding," the brigadier remembered. "I believed it was receding toward Dinwiddie."

Warren agreed. The noise level indicated heavy combat, the fading volume a Union retreat. Then two cavalry troopers, "an officer and a sergeant," reached him at 5:50 p.m. after being "cut off . . . by the enemy." Southern "cavalry and infantry" had attacked Sheridan "about noon" and tumbled his cavalry south toward Dinwiddie Courthouse, the troopers reported.

Mulling this information, Warren discussed with Chamberlain a proper response. I expressed the opinion that Grant was looking out for Sheridan," Chamberlian recalled, and if help was needed, Nelson Miles and his II Corps division "would be more likely" to march. Yet "I thought it quite probable that we should be blamed" if V Corps did not respond, he said.

Now hearing "cannonading . . . from near Dinwiddie Court-House," Warren ordered Griffin

to send Bartlett and all but three of his 3rd Brigade's nine regiments to get behind the Confederate troops battling Sheridan. Commanded by Brig. Gen. Alfred L. Pearson, the other three regiments guarded V Corps' artillery, "left on that [Boydton Plank] road on account of the mud."

Accompanied by Warren aide Maj. E. B. Cope, Bartlett started on a road that ran from the White Oak Road southwest toward the J. Boisseau house on the Crump Road above Dinwiddie Courthouse. Bartlett marched three miles before striking Confederate pickets; "some skirmishing occurred," and darkness halted further movement, Griffin said.

"Just after sunset," Chamberlain and Warren (Griffin also may have been along) "crept on our hands and knees" to V Corps' picket posts less than 200 yards from "the enemy's works, near the angle of the Claiborne Road." Union pickets caused "some stir," and Confederates "opened with musketry and artillery."

"That salient was well fortified," Chamberlain concluded.

He and Edgar M. Gregory, the 2nd Brigade commander, prowled "the picket line nearly all the night," and Griffin appeared often, "wide awake as we were."

"It was an anxious night along that front," Chamberlain admitted.

As he and Gregory reconnoitered, a communicatory hell descended on Warren and V Corps. By 6:30 p.m., Grant and Webb learned that Confederate infantry stood between Sheridan and Warren. Send Bartlett "down the Boydton plank road" as soon as possible, Webb ordered Warren.

Realizing Bartlett would need "two hours at least" to turn around and reach the road, Warren sent Pearson and his three regiments "right down toward Dinwiddie Court-House" around 6:30 p.m. Pearson reached rain-swollen and unfordable Gravelly Run, saw the Confederate-burned bridge, and stopped.

Warren had relocated his headquarters to where the military telegraph ended on the Boydton Plank Road. An 8:40 p.m. "confidential" telegram from Webb warned that "we will have to contract our lines to-night."

A 9:17 p.m. telegram from Grant (per Webb) ordered Warren to pull V Corps "back at once" to Boydton Plank Road. "Send Griffin's division" to support Sheridan, it read.

Immigrant Gustavus Sniper co-owned a cigar-making business before he enlisted as a captain in the 101st New York. Erected in 1905, a statue of Sniper and his horse "Bill" stands on Salina Street in Sniper's adopted hometown of Syracuse, New York. (oha)

Without confirming the reality on the ground, Grant abandoned White Oak Road. The battle that had cost V Corps 1,407 casualties had been fought for naught. Chamberlain would chew on that decision all his life.

With the 1st Division tucked against Confederate earthworks, Warren started Romeyn Ayres and his 2nd Division first, followed by Sam Crawford and his 3rd Division on that "stormy, starless night." An engineer, Capt. William H. H. Benyaurd, took V Corps' pioneers to build "a span of forty feet" to reopen the "broken" Gravelly Run bridge.

Then an 11:45 p.m. message from Meade told Warren to utilize the Vaughan Road and the Boydton Plank Road to reach Sheridan. Saving him was all that mattered.

The American Battlefield Trust has preserved a large swath of the White Oak Road battlefield, including original Confederate earthworks. (bfs)

Telegrams flew all night, Chamberlain and Griffin quietly pulled the 1st Division back from White Oak Road, Ayres and the 2nd Division reached Sheridan "before daybreak," and Warren came south with his other divisions. Then came the 6:00 a.m., April 1 telegram from Meade, placing Warren and V Corps under Sheridan's command.

"Orders and entreaties came fast and thick" that night "for Fifth Corps to . . . rush back five miles to the rear . . . to help Sheridan stay where Pickett and Fitz Hugh Lee had put him," Chamberlain sniffed. "Instead of the cavalry coming to help us complete our victories at the front, we were to go to the rescue of Sheridan at the rear."

Leading 1st Division, Chamberlain met Sheridan and his "weird battle-flag" at Gravelly Run. Fifth Corps soon coalesced "on the ground the enemy had occupied the evening before," and Sheridan took his combined command north toward Five Forks.

Ironically, Warren had relieved Sheridan hours earlier. Fitzhugh Lee, the Confederate cavalry commander, acknowledged that the Confederates perched "in rear of the left" of V Corps late on March 31. "Ascertaining during the night" that Warren "had about-faced and was marching" to

In December 1893, Joshua Chamberlain read his report about the White Oak Road battle to the Military Order of the Loyal Legion, Commandery of Maine. (rfl)

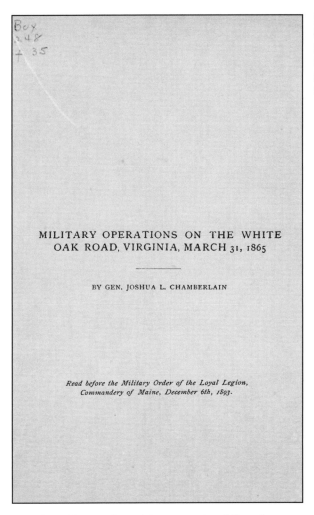

MILITARY OPERATIONS ON THE WHITE
OAK ROAD, VIRGINIA, MARCH 31, 1865

BY GEN. JOSHUA L. CHAMBERLAIN

*Read before the Military Order of the Loyal Legion,
Commandery of Maine, December 6th, 1893.*

help Sheridan and would soon arrive "directly upon our left flank," the Southerners retreated toward Five Forks "at daylight."

"It was Bartlett's outstretched line in their rear" in the gloomy dark that convinced the enemy to withdraw, Chamberlain said.

On the Road
Past Five Forks

CHAPTER TEN
APRIL 1-8, 1865

"A considerable halt" occurred Saturday morning—April 1—as Maj. Gen. Phil Sheridan's cavalry probed Confederate defenses at Five Forks. The sun glowed warmly; Union infantrymen wrung out water-logged clothing, as Chamberlain described it, "let the sun shine ... delete "Brig. Gen. Joshua L. Chamberlain observed."

He and Maj. Gen. Charles Griffin chatted, the latter alerting the former "that Grant had given Sheridan authority" to sack Warren. Talk turned to both major generals and Grant's expectations of them.

After resting "about four hours . . . we were ordered forward," Chamberlain said. In a start-and-stop march often impeded by Yankee cavalry, the V Corps took "about two hours" to "get . . . where Sheridan wants us."

Turning V Corps right (north) onto the Gravelly Run Church Road from the Courthouse Road, Warren spread his divisions in a west-to-east line of battle facing north. Romeyn Ayres and his 2nd Division formed on the left, west of the road, Sam Crawford and his 3rd Division in the center, south of Gravelly Run Church. Griffin shook out his 1st Division on the right (east).

Brigadier General Joseph Bartlett and his 3rd Brigade formed Griffin's left flank. Deployed "in three lines," 1st Brigade held the center, and Brig. Gen. Edgar Gregory and his 2nd Brigade were "placed on

An information sign identifies the White Oak Road site where Confederate earthworks angled northward near Five Forks. (bfs)

Barring access to the Southside Railroad, Confederate infantry held crucial Five Forks on April 1, 1865. Phil Sheridan decided to attack. (bfs)

the right flank of lines," Chamberlain noted. East of the 2nd Brigade roamed Union cavalry commanded by Brig. Gen. Raynald Mackenzie.

Angry that Warren's infantry was not yet all positioned—Ayres caught criticism for "the lateness of his column"—the "dark and tense" Sheridan met with Warren and his division commanders about 4:00 p.m. Bartlett and Chamberlain watched.

"Sheridan took a saber or scabbard" and drew his attack plan "on the light earth," Chamberlain said. Confederate earthworks stretched "nearly a mile westward" from Five Forks to "about three-quarters of a mile eastward," where "the extreme left [flank]" turned "northerly" for some 150 yards. Union cavalry would attack the Confederates' "right front" while V Corps hit the "left and rear." Ayres would strike the angle where the earthworks turned north, and Crawford and Griffin would outflank the angle and hit the enemy from behind.

"This was perfectly clear," Chamberlain thought.

The modern Five Forks crossroads is formed by the White Oak Road, the Courthouse Road, and the Wheeler's Pond Road. (bfs)

What Sheridan's reconnaissance did not reveal was that at the angle, V Corps would face Brig. Gen. Matthew W. Ransom and his North Carolina brigade, reinforced by artillery. To Ransom's right (west) along the White Oak Road entrenchments spread the South Carolinians commanded by Brig. Gen. William H. Wallace, and Brig. Gen. George H. Steuart and his Virginians held the earthworks on Wallace's right flank.

The conferees rejoined their commands. Brigadier General Frederick Winthrop, whose brigade had suffered so terribly in Friday's fighting, rode to

Chamberlain and asked, "Dear old fellow, have you managed to bring up anything to eat?" He had eaten "scarcely a mouthful to-day."

A Chamberlain orderly "hurried up whatever we had," and the brigadiers "sat there on a log" and ate some rations. In those last minutes before the fight, "it was a homely scene and humblest; but ever to be held in memory," Chamberlain recalled.

The V Corps stepped off to commence the Battle of Five Forks at 4:00 p.m. Suddenly, Warren dispensed a confusing diagram and orders to his generals. The diagram, apparently based on Sheridan's, placed the Confederate earthworks south of White Oak Road and crossing it at the Gravelly Run Church Road intersection. An arrow drawn on the diagram directed V Corps to steer northwest, with Griffin actually behind Crawford, directly into the enemy's defenses.

Representing the artillery sprinkled along George Pickett's White Oak Road earthworks, a rifled cannon stands at Five Forks. (bfs)

Warren's order indicated that his divisions "will swing around to the left[,] perpendicular to the White Oak Road" and "get engaged" with the Confederate earthworks.

Believing the concept "a thing absurd to conceive," Chamberlain sought clarification from Griffin. "We will not worry ourselves about diagrams," he said. "We are to follow Crawford," who headed north.

Its alignment disintegrated as V Corps reached White Oak Road. Crawford drifted slightly to the east and, once over the road, angled 45 degrees to the northwest and shifted unnoticed to Griffin's right flank. Crawford's men plowed "through bogs, tangled woods, and thickets of pine, interspersed with open spaces here and there."

The 1st Division pivoted 45 degrees to the left below White Oak Road and interposed between the other two divisions. Chamberlain suddenly realized that neither Bartlett nor Crawford were on the 1st Brigade's left flank. Then shooting broke out on the right where Crawford "encountered the enemy's skirmishers."

"A sudden burst of fire exactly on our left" got Chamberlain's attention, too. "That could only be from Ayres's attack."

Ayres had crossed White Oak Road after chasing off Southern skirmishers. Gunfire erupting on his left flank, he swung two brigades into line facing west, "pushed forward, and soon" struck the angle, "covered by a strong breast-work . . . about 100 yards in length." His men charged with the cold steel.

Halting his brigade off to the northeast, Chamberlain rode "to some high, cleared ground" on the Sydnor field to study the action. Across the field, Crawford engaged in "strong skirmishing." To the south, 600 yards from the 3rd Division, "Ayres's troops" swirled in heavy combat. His corps flag visible, Warren rode toward Crawford, and Griffin and his flag appeared near Ayres.

Seeing Griffin in the distance "was enough order for me" concluded Chamberlain as he maneuvered his brigade to support Ayres.

Riding onto Sydnor field, Joe Bartlett saw Griffin and the fighting, too. He swung into line the 1st Michigan, 20th Maine, and 151st Pennsylvania, "wheeled them sharp to the left, and charged."

With Bartlett now on his right flank, Chamberlain took his 1st Brigade "rapidly under the crest of a hill and charged the [enemy's] works, striking them obliquely in flank and reverse." Gustavus Sniper and the 185th New York, along with Maj. Edwin A. Glenn and half of the 198th Pennsylvania, attacked along the inside of the earthworks, the other 198th companies along the outside.

The U.S. Department of the Interior placed this monument declaring Five Forks a Registered National Historic Landmark on the battlefield in 1961. (bfs)

Chamberlain promised Glenn a colonelcy if his men captured the defenses. "Boys, will you follow me?" Glenn yelled. "A deadly struggle ensued" at the earthworks; on the fourth attempt the 198th's flag "floated triumphant over the works," said Maj. E. Morrison Woodward.

Watching Glenn take the 198th "into the hurricane of fire," Chamberlain rode over to congratulate him. "I met two men bearing his body,—the dripping blood marking their path." The soldiers identified Glenn as mortally wounded. Stopping beside them, Chamberlain leaned from the saddle. "General, I have carried out your wishes!" Glenn exclaimed.

Heartbroken, Chamberlain leaned closer and said, "*Colonel*, I will remember my promise; I will remember *you*!" After the battle he sent "my recommendation for two brevets" for Glenn, afterwards known as "'Brevet Colonel.'"

Late in forming his 2nd Division for the Five Forks attack, Romeyn Ayres incurred Phil Sheridan's criticism on April 1. (loc)

Forming to counterattack, desperate Confederates "began to press us hard on the right flank," said the 20th Maine's commander, Lt. Col. Walter G. Morrill, sending Maj. Atherton W. Clark and then another officer to alert Bartlett. "The enemy . . . continued to press us very hard, and we were losing men fast."

"It was hot work . . . in many places it was a hand-to-hand fight," said Pvt. Theodore Gerrish, Co. H, 20th Maine. "Clubbed muskets came crashing down . . . upon human skulls," and "men were bayoneted in cold blood."

Noticing the "very heavy flank fire" affecting Bartlett's brigade and its "extreme right falling back," Chamberlain and other senior officers undertook "the utmost personal efforts" to rally the troops. Bartlett requested help, and Chamberlain hurled two regiments behind the 20th Maine and 1st Michigan to break the attack. That sweep "relieved us at once," Morrill said.

Chamberlain and Bartlett rounded up and pushed forward "the stragglers . . . 150 or 200" sheltering at a tree line. Gregory and his brigade plunged into the fight, as did Brig. Gen. James Gwyn and his brigade from the 2nd Division. Fred Winthrop went down mortally wounded while leading his command; Chamberlain would mourn him and Glenn.

The fighting "was a whirl. Every way was front, and every way was flank," Chamberlain realized. Hundreds of Confederates suddenly rushed through

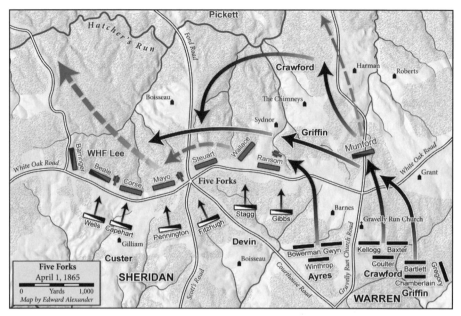

Five Forks
April 1, 1865
0   Yards   1,000
Map by Edward Alexander

FIVE FORKS, APRIL 1, 1865— While his cavalry attacked Five Forks head-on, Phil Sheridan envisioned V Corps hitting the enemy lines where the Confederate earthworks angled north near the White Oak Road-Gravelly Run Church Road intersection. The actual angle lay farther west, and the error disrupted the Union infantry's advance.

a gap; expecting an attack, the brigadier rode into "my left battalion" and shouted, "Prepare to fire by the rear rank!"

His men spun around. "We surrender!" shouted the Southerners, dropping their weapons and lifting their hands and "running right in upon us."

The fighting continued. "The whole line pressed on, three brigades of the division as one," driving the enemy "I should judge . . . a mile or more," Chamberlain recalled.

As Southern resistance faded, Romeyn Ayres and his division "pushed forward rapidly . . . till dark, over some three miles," capturing "some 2,000 prisoners and 8 battle-flags."

Sam Crawford and his 3rd Division pushed on through the rough terrain north of White Oak Road and reached "the enemy's rear on the Ford road, which I crossed." He was sending "many prisoners" and captured transportation "to the rear" when Confederates "opened upon my center and left flank a very heavy fire."

Warren swept up and ordered an "advance immediately down the Ford road" toward Five Forks, and Crawford went with Brig. Gen. Richard Coulter and his 3rd Brigade. Overrunning a four-gun artillery battery and killing its commander, the Yankees sent "the enemy flying before us" before reaching and capturing earthworks near Five Forks.

Still unsatisfied with what he saw as Warren's reluctant movements to support him, Sheridan sacked the V Corps commander and replaced him on the field with Charles Griffin. Informed by the latter's aide amidst the fighting, "I was astonished at first, and incredulous afterwards," Chamberlain said. He soon ran into Warren, now without a command.

Union troops had pushed west beyond Five Forks as darkness descended. A last Southern stand had briefly checked the Yankees, so Griffin told Lt. Col. Hollon Richardson to advance his 7th Wisconsin. With that regiment went Warren, holding "his corps flag" as he and Richardson rode over the enemy's earthworks. Perhaps Warren sought death, but it found Richardson, struck down shielding Warren and spraying the regimental "colors with his blood," Chamberlain recalled.

The enemy faded into the night. Officially relieved by written order and Sheridan snark, Warren rode into history. Griffin had Chamberlain pull together the scattered 1st Division, done by a hard ride and repetitive bugle calls. The battle of Five Forks was over and Pickett's division had been destroyed by the relentless assaults

The ill-fated Frederick Winthrop shared a soldier's repast with Joshua Chamberlain shortly before Five Forks. (loc)

The battle won, Chamberlain claimed his brigade took "nearly 900" prisoners and four battle flags, one torn apart by its followers and squirreled into their pockets.

*   *   *

With Union cavalry pursuing defeated Confederates "out of sight and hearing" late on April Fool's Day, Griffin halted the V Corps on the Five Forks battlefield. Sheridan then ordered the corps

Gravelly Run Church Road (foreground) divided V Corps, which advanced across the White Oak Road intersection. (bfs)

Trees grow from the earthworks marking where the Confederate angle turned north, away from White Oak Road. (bfs)

Joining the army as a surgeon in 1851, Samuel Crawford was the Fort Sumter surgeon a decade later. He soon transferred to the infantry. (loc)

consolidated about three miles away "near Gravelly Run Church," said Griffin.

On Sunday morning, April 2, Sheridan shifted the V Corps two miles farther eastward to help the II Corps' division of Brig. Gen. Nelson A. Miles attack the enemy's Claiborne Road defenses. Farther east, Union troops had already made their "splendid and triumphant assault" on the outer Southern lines at Petersburg, noted Chamberlain.

Shortly after 9:00 a.m., Maj. Gen. Andrew A. Humphreys and his II Corps rolled across White Oak Road to scour away the defenders and push toward Sutherland's Station on the Southside Railroad. Humphreys called away Miles, so Sheridan promptly turned around the redundant V Corps, which started marching toward Five Forks at 11:00 a.m.

"What lost labor for Miles and the Fifth Corps, running empty express up and down the White Oak Road!" Chamberlain groused.

Not until afternoon did the leading 1st Division probe north on the Ford Road, called "Church road" by Chamberlain, his brigade forming the vanguard. Gustavus Sniper and his 185th New York drove off Confederate cavalry disputing the Hatcher's Run crossing. Reinforced by the 32nd Massachusetts (Lt. Col. James A. Cunningham), the New Yorkers splashed across the "small creek" and approached Cox's Station on the Southside Railroad.

A train approached from Petersburg, and Chamberlain "pushed forward our skirmishers to capture it." They did, and Cunningham celebrated by pulling "the whistle-valve wide open," the "wild shriek" announcing the locomotive's "arrival at a premature station."

The 1st Brigade had cut the railroad. "This train was crowded with quite a mixed company as to color, character, and capacity," observed Chamberlain. Confederate soldiers became prisoners while the civilian pedestrians were "let go in peace, if they could find it."

Now commanding the 1st Division, Joseph Bartlett sent the 1st Brigade north to the Cox Road intersection, defended by "about 1,500 dismounted cavalry" deployed in a single line, estimated Chamberlain. Decades later he upped that number to "about ten thousand men."

Forward went the 1st Brigade, with Capt. John Stanton leading the 198th Pennsylvania. Through the woods on Chamberlain's right flank maneuvered the 189th New York (Lt. Col. Joseph G. Townsend). Delivering a "brisk fire," the Union infantry lost only three men wounded while clearing the field.

Sheridan arrived, pointed east on the Cox Road, and the 1st Brigade tramped parallel to the railroad before stopping at a Hatcher's Run tributary (probably Crandle's Run) "a mile short of Sutherland's" Station, Chamberlain recalled. His brigade stood guard as V Corps' uniformed vandals tore apart the tracks from Cox's Station to his position.

The V Corps then moved east to occupy "the intersection of Namozine road with the River road," Griffin recalled. Two divisions bivouacked around "the Williamson house" while Brig. Gen. Samuel W. Crawford took his 3rd Division northwest on the Namozine Road to support Union cavalry fighting Confederates near a destroyed bridge over Namozine Creek.

Under heavy fire from Confederate defenders, a V Corps battle line charges the Southern earthworks near Five Forks on April 1. (loc)

Several Union infantrymen guard Confederates captured at Five Forks. The battle destroyed George Pickett's division. (loc)

With Confederate troops moving west after abandoning Petersburg and Richmond, Lt. Gen. Ulysses S. Grant ordered a hot pursuit. Sheridan pushed his cavalry ahead of the V Corps, and the hard-marching infantry followed "the Namozine road toward Amelia Court-House" or took "the River Road," according to Chamberlain.

Marching by dawn on Tuesday, April 4, the 1st Division reached the Richmond & Danville Railroad south of Jetersville by dark, dug in, and waited. "The enemy appeared in force" as, intent on turning southwest toward North Carolina, Robert E. Lee consolidated his retreating army at Jetersville.

"We were pretty sure to be ourselves attacked with desperation in the [Wednesday] morning," Chamberlain said.

Conferring with his cavalry commanders, Lee hesitated to attack. The II Corps appeared at 2:30 p.m., April 5 and gradually formed on V Corps' left flank. Up came the foot-sore VI Corps to take the right flank. The "Army of the Potomac [was] together once again," Chamberlain realized.

Later that night, Sheridan returned V Corps to the "seriously ill" Maj. Gen. George G. Meade, and Griffin met with him about dark. Stepping out at 6:00 a.m., Thursday, the V Corps pushed up the railroad to find enemy positions abandoned and evidence that Lee "had gone westward," Griffin said. The corps briefly halted until receiving new orders from Meade, then advanced north "to move on the right of the army" so that VI Corps could shift to the left and join Sheridan, its commander from the Valley campaign.

"Capturing about 300 prisoners and many wagons," Griffin pushed his divisions 32 miles through Paineville to Ligontown Ferry. Exhausted soldiers collapsed where they stopped after dark.

The pursuit continued through Friday, April 7, with the V Corps tramping "for High Bridge, via Rice's Store," Griffin reported. At 9:30 a.m. he received orders to cut behind II and VI corps, reach Prince Edward Courthouse before day's end, and form the left flank with XXIV Corps. The V Corps covered 20 miles that day.

"On the 8th we moved by way of Prospect Station up the Lynchburg pike," Chamberlain said. The march continued into the night. Everywhere his men passed a disintegrating army's (and nation's) detritus: wheeled military and civilian vehicles abandoned in deep mud, starving mules or horses still in harness; scarecrow-thin soldiers dead along roadsides; and "wild-looking men in homespun gray" claiming they were either civilians or, despite their epidermal hue, "not white, but colored." The lies usually failed, and the two army corps took more prisoners.

While crossing the Buffalo River, Chamberlain let Charlemagne "take a drink." The horse stepped into a deep channel, leaving mount and rider swimming until they reached a miry shore. Chamberlain hinted at the mirth stifled by the "two or three" soldiers helping him and Charlemagne to solid footing.

Darkness hampered mobility, the repetitive start-and-stop of weary XXIV Corps frustrated Griffin, yet V Corps tramped 29 miles to bivouac around 2:00 a.m., Sunday, April 9, about two miles from Appomattox Courthouse, Griffin reported.

Perhaps seeking death and glory, Gouverneur K. Warren participated in the sunset charge at Five Forks after Phil Sheridan relieved him of V Corps command. (loc)

Little remained other than railroad-car axles and wheels after Union cavalry captured and burned a Confederate train on the Southside Railroad at Appomattox Station on April 8, 1865. (loc)

FROM THIS SPOT WAS FIRED
LAST SHOT FROM THE ARTILLARY
OF THE ARMY OF NOTHERN VIRGINIA.
ON THE MORNING OF APRIL 9TH.
1865.

So Ended that 9th of April, 1865

CHAPTER ELEVEN
APRIL 9 - 12, 1865

The dog-tired Brig. Gen. Joshua L. Chamberlain dreamed in the Palm Sunday darkness. Somewhere outside his exhausted body, a familiar sound gradually strengthened: a horse, ridden hard, rapidly nearing the 1st Brigade's rough bivouac south of Appomattox Court House.

Chamberlain's hearing relayed the vision: a cavalry trooper hurtling from the saddle to pull "from his jacket-front a crumpled note" that he handed to "the sentinel standing watch."

"Orders, sir, I think," the weary infantryman said while touching his general's shoulder.

Pushing upward with an elbow, Chamberlain struck a match and "read the brief, thrilling note, sent back by Maj. Gen. Phil Sheridan to us infantry commanders." Union cavalry had captured three Confederate trains at nearby Appomattox Station. Sheridan now blocked the retreating Confederate army; "if you can possibly push your infantry up here to-night, we will have great results in the morning," he promised.

Bugles blared through the V Corps, which quickly formed before starting to march at 4:00 a.m. Chamberlain's brigade took the van and reached Appomattox Station by dawn. Sheridan had left a staff officer who right-turned the brigade north toward Appomattox Court House, the village through which Maj. Gen. John B. Gordon had pushed Confederate infantry that same morning to clear away Union cavalry blocking the Lynchburg Stage Road, which Chamberlain called the "Lynchburg Pike."

A bronze tablet near the Peers House at Appomattox Court House indicates where a Confederate gun crew fired the last shot by the Army of Northern Virginia. (bfs)

Ahead of Gordon advanced Maj. Gen. Fitzhugh
Lee's Southern cavalrymen. Men bled and died on
this April 9, "one of those soft gray-and-green April
mornings with clouds over the rising sun, but with
foliage seeming to reflect a luminous warmth of spring,"
noted future 20th Maine biographer John J. Pullen.

Moving at the double quick in separate corps
columns, Union infantry legged toward the fighting.
Major General Edward O. C. Ord had brought his
Army of the James, comprising XXIV Corps (Maj.
Gen. John Gibbon) and XXV Corps (Maj. Gen.
Godfrey Weitzel) on the epic tramp from Petersburg.
Black regiments filled Weitzel's two divisions.

Hustling along with Co. M, 198th Pennsylvania,
Sgt. John W. Burnett first saw "Ord's colored troops"
while approaching Appomattox Station. The black
soldiers "suddenly . . . approached the front of ours
from our left rear, marching on the same road with
us . . . in the southwest corner of the large open
field where" Sheridan "gave Gen. Chamberlain his
orders." Avoiding the field, "the colored troops . . .
continued on north on this road, which would bring
them west of the Courthouse soon," Burnett recalled.

Chamberlain's ears sorted the combat: "the sharp
ring of the horse-artillery, answered . . . by heavier
field guns," cavalry carbines "cracking" and infantry
rifles roaring, the noise "drawing nearer."

"It has come at last,—the supreme hour,"
Chamberlain realized.

With his brigade now "about in the middle of our
Fifth Corps column," he responded immediately when
"a cavalry staff officer" suddenly appeared and said,
"General Sheridan wishes you to break off from this
column and come to his support . . . act on this at once."

Dispatching an aide to tell his division commander—
Maj. Gen. Charles Griffin—Chamberlain peeled off
the 1st and 2nd brigades. Sheridan's aide explained
that while Ord's infantry had stopped the Confederates
on the stage road, the enemy's left now maneuvered
"to cut through near the Court House." Sheridan had
aligned Brig. Gen. Thomas C. Devin's 1st Division,
Cavalry Corps, to meet the threat.

Emerging from some woods, Chamberlain
encountered Sheridan astride his "grim charger,
Rienzi." Forward, Sheridan gestured without

speaking. The 1st Brigade deployed into two lines. Brigadier General Edgar M. Gregory formed his 2nd Brigade similarly on Chamberlain's left flank, and "our lines advanced against the enemy, relieving the cavalry, who reformed on my right.

"The skirmishers drove the enemy rapidly . . . while our line of battle was opened on by a battery in the town," Chamberlain reported. Retreating uphill, enemy infantry occupied a stone wall, but "a light artillery" fire shoved them away. Chamberlain advanced his brigades, "and on the crest we stood."

"One booming cannon-shot passed close along our front, and in the next moment all was still," he noticed.

Off to the left, Ord's divisions blocked the stage road. The V Corps formed on the right flank. Maybe "five miles away, II and VI corps closed on Robert E. Lee and his hungry army from the east.

"Their last hope is gone," Chamberlain believed.

The "hilly, broken ground" creating "a vast amphitheater," he and other Union soldiers looked into a valley occupied by Lee's army, infantry "suddenly resting in place" and "clouds of cavalry" milling aimlessly. Then north by northeast went the V Corps line, advancing "down a little slope, through a swamp, over a bright swift stream."

"Their skirmishers fell back fighting, the batteries open, the Court House is gained, and fighting commences in the streets," remembered Maj. E. Morrison Woodward, the 198th Pennsylvania's historian.

"There is wild work, that looks like fighting," Chamberlain noticed, "but not much killing, nor even hurting . . . a wild, mild fussing."

He saw both a rider moving between the lines and the Union cavalry ejecting a rider who joined the first horseman. "Nearly a mile away," the men headed "towards our position." Yet a third horseman, "a Confederate staff officer undoubtedly," appeared nearer the 1st Brigade while carrying a white flag, actually "a towel, and one so white," Chamberlain realized.

Seeing the brigadier's battle flag, the officer (Capt. P. M. Jones) dismounted, saluted Chamberlain, and said, "Sir, I am from General Gordon. General Lee desires a cessation of hostilities until he can hear from General Grant as to the proposed surrender."

Edward O. C. Ord witnessed the official surrender ceremony inside the McLean house. (loc)

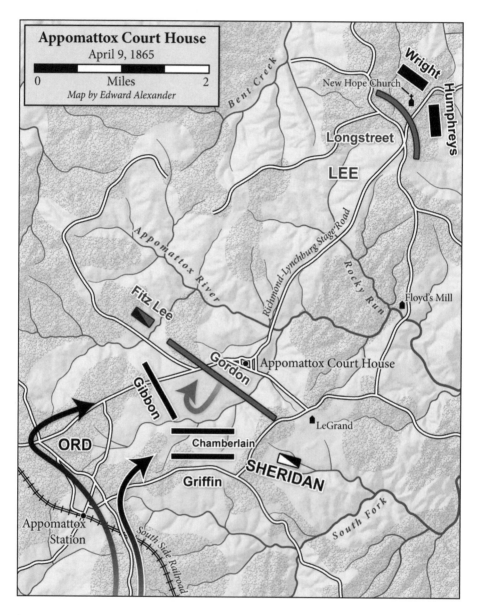

APPOMATTOX COURT HOUSE, APRIL 9, 1865—Marching alongside Edward O. C. Ord's Army of the James, the V Corps of Charles Griffin swung into line to block John Gordon's advancing Confederates in mid-morning. Phil Sheridan and his cavalry blocked a possible flank maneuver by Gordon.

"Sir, that matter exceeds my authority," Chamberlain replied. "I will send to my superior. General Lee is right. He can do no more."

Unaware that Ulysses S. Grant had traded messages with Lee these past days, Chamberlain awaited Griffin's orders. The two approaching riders coalesced as Lt. Col. Edward W. Whitaker, chief of staff for Brig. Gen. George A. Custer, and a "Capt. Brown of Georgia." Whitaker carried a white flag.

As Whitaker later explained, Custer "was about to order a charge" when Capt. R. M. Sims, an aide to Lt. Gen. James Longstreet, "met us" and reported that Lee sought a ceasefire. Custer sent Whitaker with Sims to tell Lee that "I can not stop this charge unless he announces an unconditional surrender."

Sims took Whitaker through the lines to Gordon and Longstreet, but Lee "had galloped off to the rear" to find Grant. The Confederate generals "assured me of an absolute surrender" and "begged me to hurry and to first stop that [approaching] infantry line with the announcement."

George Custer and his cavalry constantly slashed and bloodied retreating Confederate formations during the Appomattox campaign. (loc)

Whitaker would "do so only" if accompanied by "a rebel officer," so Gordon sent Brown.

The two riders "steared for what appeared to be the [infantry] commander's flag (Chamberlain's brigade flag)," Whitaker recalled. "I understood the officer to be yourself commanding that portion of General Ord's line."

"This is unconditional surrender! This is the end!" Whitaker shouted before passing along Gordon's request that a senior officer halt the advancing Union troops, "or hell will be to pay!

"You were the first person to receive the announcement of the unconditional surrender of General Lee's army at Appomattox Court House," Whitaker later told Chamberlain. "The moment the surrender was announced[,] the greatest[,] loudest cheers I ever heard went up from right to left along your line." Whitaker rode to find Sheridan, and Brown stayed with Chamberlain.

Shooting occurred in the distance, and near the Peers house on the village's eastern end, a Confederate cannon fired. The shell exploded amidst some 1st Brigade skirmishers and struck down Lt. Hiram Clark of Co. G, 185th New York.

Chamberlain thought him "the last man killed [in combat] in the Army of the Potomac," but perhaps not the last Union soldier killed at Appomattox Court House. "The honor of this last death is not a proper subject of quarrel," he wrote years later.

The initial truce expired at 1:00 p.m.; lacking an official surrender notification, Union generals planned to attack. Then Lee—"a commanding form, superbly mounted, richly accoutered," Chamberlain said—rode between the lines. Clad in a "slouched hat without cord; common soldier's blouse; high boots, mud-splashed to the top," Grant soon approached on "another . . . road." The generals signed the surrender documents in Wilmer McLean's parlor, and Lee rode away on Traveller.

The "modern" Appomattox Court House replicates the two-story brick courthouse built in 1846 and destroyed by fire in 1892. Lee's surrender might have taken place inside the courthouse had it not been closed on Palm Sunday 1865.
(bfs)

"Lee surrenders!" shouted staff officers riding through the Union formations. Later that day, Union soldiers sent rations to the "starving" Confederates; Chamberlain wryly noted the provisions included Confederate rations captured by Sheridan's troopers at Appomattox Station.

"And so ended that 9th of April, 1865—Palm Sunday,—in that obscure little Virginia village now blazoned for immortal fame," said Chamberlain.

* * *

Summoned to army headquarters at Appomattox Court House early on Tuesday, April 11, Chamberlain met with major generals Charles Griffin and John Gibbon, "two of the three senior officers" named by Grant to oversee dismantling the Army of Northern Virginia. Major General Wesley Merritt, the third officer, was away.

Chamberlain learned that Lee was en route to Richmond, Grant to City Point. The latter wanted the Confederate infantry to surrender in "a formal

Charles Raine built in 1848 the two-story brick house that Wilmer McLean purchased in 1863. (loc)

ceremony" by marching past Union troops "to lay down their arms and colors."

Grant put Chamberlain in "charge of this parade and . . . the formal surrender," Griffin and Gibbon said.

Realizing that the surrender would "be a crowning incident of history," Chamberlain asked Griffin "for my old Third Brigade, which I had commanded after Gettysburg."

Their ranks combat-thinned since March 29, the men were "veterans, and replaced veterans," the older regiments "cut to pieces, cut down, consolidated," Chamberlain said. "I thought these veterans deserved this recognition."

Army bureaucracy churned out the requisite paperwork. "The general commanding having been ordered to another command hereby takes leave of this brigade," the 1st Brigade boys learned from General Order No. 3 after daylight on April 11. Chamberlain praised his New York and Pennsylvania warriors "for their fidelity and courtesy" and expressed his "pride" for "their soldierly behavior and gallant conduct in battle."

That morning, Maj. Gen. Joseph Bartlett shifted the 1st Division to replace a XXIV Corps division at Appomattox Court House. He also released the 1st and 2nd brigades to participate in the Wednesday surrender.

Flowing through a valley, the Appomattox River separated the Confederates camping along the northern hills from the Union troops bivouacked nearer Appomattox Court House. The Lynchburg Stage Road, called by Chamberlain "the principal street of the town," angled northeast beyond the village and ran downhill to cross the river.

On April 9 Confederate troops camped on the distant hills visible along the horizon northeast of Appomattox Court House. (bfs)

Turning out before dawn on Wednesday, April 12, "a chill gray morning," the 1st Division deployed along the stage road, "from the bluff bank of the stream to near the Court House on the left," observed Chamberlain.

The 3rd Brigade formed along the road's southern edge and faced north. From right to left (east to west) stood the 32nd Massachusetts, the 1st Battalion Maine Sharpshooters, the 20th Maine, the 1st and 16th Michigan, and the 83rd, 91st, 118th, and 155th Pennsylvanians.

The 2nd Brigade stood in battle line behind the 3rd, and the 1st Brigade faced south along the road's northern edge after forming opposite the 3rd Brigade. The division's left flank ended

Union infantrymen pose with their "stands of arms" outside Appomattox Court House. (loc)

"near the fence" enclosing the McLean house yard, said a soldier in the 118th Pennsylvania (the "Corn Exchange Regiment"), on the 3rd Brigade's left flank.

The 1st Division boys "had spruced up . . . and arms, accoutrements and clothing showed but little of the rough usage" from "this hard campaign," he noticed.

"With my staff" and a flagbearer carrying "the old flag—the red maltese cross on a white field with blue border, I took post on the right" at 5 a.m., Chamberlain said. One Maine soldier claimed the 1st Division formed by 9:00 a.m.

Astride Charlemagne, Chamberlain waited with his staff on the extreme right flank, "nearest the Rebel soldiers who were approaching our right." His infantry stood at "order arms" as the Confederate van "started down into the valley . . . and approached our lines."

"Ah, but it was a most impressive sight, a most striking picture, to see that whole army in motion . . .," and by the battered battle flags, "the old 'Stonewall' Jackson Brigade" led, he decided.

Major General John B. Gordon rode in front as his Second Corps marched "to . . . where its arms were to be stacked." After ascending the hill toward Appomattox Court House, his men "moved in front of the division commanded by that knightly soldier, General Joshua L. Chamberlain, of Maine."

"That brilliant officer called his command into line and saluted the Confederates at a 'present arms' as they filed by, a final and fitting tribute of Northern chivalry to Southern courage," Gordon said.

Southern infantry crossed the Appomattox River below Appomattox Court House while en route to surrender their weapons on April 12. (bfs)

Chamberlain watched the approaching Gordon, "his chin drooped to his breast, downhearted and dejected in appearance almost beyond description." A Union bugle blew as Gordon "came opposite me," and the Yankees came to attention, regiment by regiment in succession.

The first Union regiment then snapped into "carry arms," the soldiers holding their rifled muskets "by the right hand and perpendicular to the shoulder," Chamberlain said. "I may best describe it as a marching salute in review."

Wheeling his horse toward Chamberlain, Gordon "gently" applied his spurs "so that the animal slightly reared, and as he wheeled, horse and rider made one motion, the horse's head swung down with a graceful bow, and General Gordon dropped his swordpoint to his toe in salutation," recalled Chamberlain.

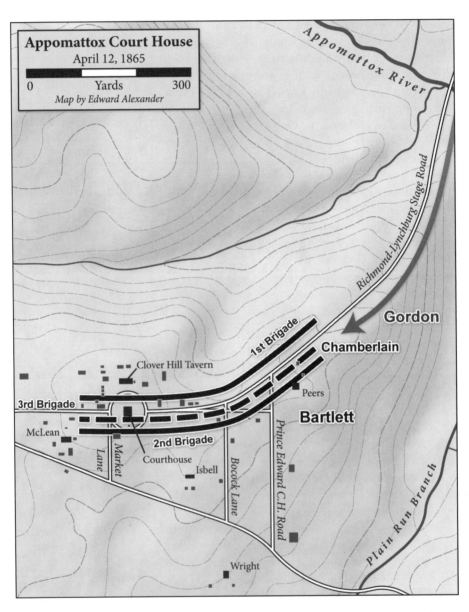

APPOMATTOX COURT HOUSE, APRIL 12, 1865—To Joshua Chamberlain went the honor of commanding the Union troops receiving the Confederate infantry's official surrender on April 12. Chamberlain spread his old 3rd Brigade along the Lynchburg Stage Road; the two other 1st Division brigades formed along his line.

Gordon ordered his worn veterans to assume "carry arms" as they passed the Union boys performing "carry arms" regiment by regiment as the Southerners passed.

Private Theodore Gerrish, Co. H, 20th Maine, thought that "as a rule they were tall, thin, spare men, with long hair and beard of a tawny red color. "All clad in . . . Southern gray," the Confederates wore "broad-brimmed, slouching gray hats" and appeared "very ragged and dirty," he commented.

Stopping about 12 feet from the Union infantry, each Confederate regiment "turned . . . toward us" in well-formed lines, "with every officer in his appointed position," Chamberlain said. "Bayonets were affixed to muskets, arms stacked, and cartridge boxes unslung and hung upon the stacks."

John Gordon served as a Georgia senator and governor after the Civil War. (loc)

Then the Confederates surrendered their "torn and tattered battleflags." He saw grizzled veterans burst "from the ranks" and, with tears coursing their cheeks, kiss "their old flags." Gordon never forgot "the briny tears that ran down the haggard and tanned faces of the starving Confederates" or "the veneration and devotion which they displayed for the tattered flags."

"Poor fellows," thought Chamberlain. "I pitied them from the bottom of my heart. Those had been well handled," the "flags bravely borne." The surrender stretched through that Tuesday. Several Confederate generals made conciliatory and friendly remarks, Chamberlain noticed.

Then Brig. Gen. Henry A. Wise approached with his First Military District division. Virginia's governor in 1859, Wise had signed the death warrant for John Brown. Their individual photographs portray men eerily sharing a zealot's focused glare, and the inveterate secessionist and the psychopathic abolitionist detested their perceived enemies. After the next few minutes, Chamberlain and many Union boys never forgot Wise.

"A small, thin man, with a red face and shrill, sharp voice," he "rode a large, powerful horse, and looked like a grim, soured, passionate man," thought Theodore Gerrish.

"I saw him fidgeting and bungling about as if he could not handle his men . . . with the knot of his handkerchief under his left ear, and tobacco juice, or some other venom, trickling from the drawn down corners of his mouth," Chamberlain observed.

When his troops halted before the 3rd Brigade, Wise thought them slow in forming their lines. "With much profanity he abused the men for being so tardy in their movements," Gerrish said. "We quickly detected . . . that he was not admired by his men" as several Confederates taunted Wise, now technically neither a general nor a soldier.

Attempting small talk, Chamberlain said that "the good order of the troops" suggested the North and South might express "future good will" toward reconciliation.

"His old habit of talking came on," noticed a correspondent watching Wise, whose big mouth snarled, "General Chamberlain, we are subjugated, but not subdued. Sir, we have here [striking his breast] hearts burning with undying hate."

"We hate you, Sir—I hate you!" Wise exclaimed.

Perhaps embarrassed by his outburst, he mentioned the two bullet holes "in the breast of my coat and a much-abused sleeve" torn up by that rambling bullet at Lewis Farm, Chamberlain recalled.

The conversation could have turned pleasant, but the vituperative Wise vented his anger, hissing that Virginia's "curse is on you." Nearby Confederate and Union staff officers laughed aloud. Watching him ride away, Chamberlain thought, "'Whom the gods love die early'; there I say long live Henry A. Wise."

He was not the only angry Confederate that day, remembered Sgt. John W. Burnett of Co. M, 198th Pennsylvania. "Some of our late adversaries were insolent in passing us . . . but among them were many who were glad as we that the end had come," he commented.

Last came Maj. Henry Kyd Douglas with his brigade, comprising five Virginia regiments. Assigned to Thomas "Stonewall" Jackson's staff in spring 1862, badly wounded and captured at Gettysburg, he was released in March 1864. Later a Gordon aide, Douglas got field command as the Appomattox campaign opened.

He "asked General Gordon to let my brigade—as it had fired the last shot—be the last to stack arms. In a little while my time came to march. My decimated and ragged band with their bullet-torn banner marched" past "a heavy line of Union soldiers" standing "opposite us in absolute silence."

Suddenly a Union soldier "called for three cheers for the last brigade to surrender." Voices erupted in

loud cheering, and "this soldierly generosity was more than we could bear," said Douglas, crying so hard that "my own eyes were as blind as my voice was dumb." His "grizzled veterans wept like women" as "that line of blue broke its respectful silence to pay such tribute . . . to the little line in grey. . . ."

Union soldiers (right and far left) watch as Confederate infantrymen lay down their arms and equipment at Appomattox Court House. (loc)

After stacking their arms, the Confederates marched to the McLean house, signed and obtained their paroles, and left Appomattox Court House, "clouds of men on foot or horse, singly or in groups," Chamberlain said.

His men recovered 17,000 firearms "and a hundred battle-flags," and the Union army issued some 27,000 paroles. With the Confederates vanquished, the 1st Division and V Corps need not linger at Appomattox Court House.

The Appomattox campaign officially spanned March 29-April 9, 1865. The V Corps suffered 2,465 casualties during those 12 days, with the 1st Division accounting for 691 men, including 100 killed, 561 wounded, and 30 missing.

With its losses split almost evenly between the 185th New York and the 198th Pennsylvania, the 1st Brigade lost 447 men: 64 killed, 330 wounded, and 28 captured or missing. Chamberlain was the only casualty among the "Staff." In his after-action report, Charles Griffin cited three general officers "for their promptness, efficiency, and zealousness in the execution of all orders."

Among the three was Brig. Gen. Joshua L. Chamberlain.

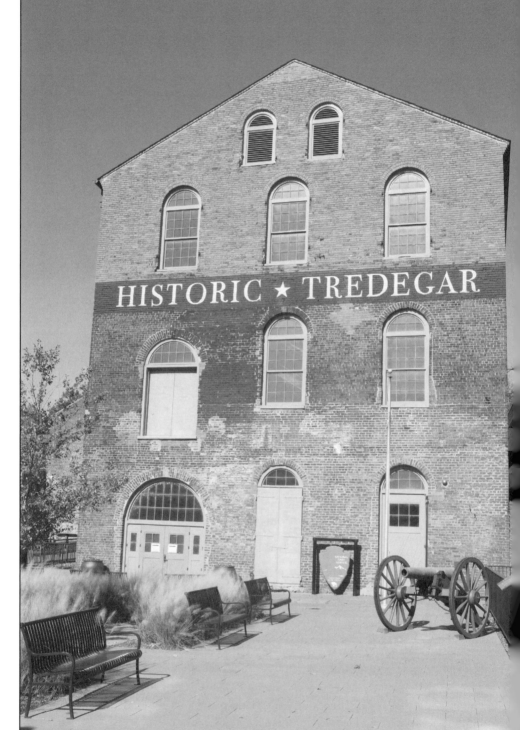

Toward Washington
They Tramped

CHAPTER TWELVE
APRIL 14 – MAY 12, 1865

Stomachs growled in the 1st Division by Good Friday 1865. Its wagon trains strung out somewhere between Jetersville and Appomattox Court House, V Corps went hungry as Holy Week passed. "The rations reduced to sediment in the haversacks smelt of lead and gunpowder," muttered Brig. Gen. Joshua L. Chamberlain.

"All hands had to forage for a living," so Yankees tramped across the countryside, often bringing back "only . . . armfuls of corn on the cob," which the men soaked in water "to yield to our practised jaws," he said.

Empty bellies went east with the V Corps on Saturday, April 15 as the vanguard left that morning for Burkeville. The 3rd Brigade stepped off at 1:00 p.m., recalled Pvt. Theodore Gerrish, 20th Maine. The column spread along the Lynchburg Stage Road, "it was raining very hard," Virginia's gloriously red mud soon splattered everyone, and "the men were hungry and consequently savage," he growled.

Regimental marching integrity disintegrated as men sought individual routes through the mud. Rain turned adjacent fields gooey, V Corps marched "until at least an hour after dark," and then word came that "some one had blundered," causing at least the 3rd Brigade to march "the last two miles in the wrong direction," Gerrish spat.

So around turned Chamberlain's men; back they went to the stage road to camp "on a low, boggy . . . ground . . . covered by stunted . . . pine trees," said

The historic buildings at Tredegar Iron Works are among the Civil War structures that survive in Richmond today. (bfs)

Gerrish, spreading his blanket across tree roots so he could sleep above the wet soil.

Easter Sunday, April 16, dawned with a "chilly rain and lowering clouds," Chamberlain recalled. His brigade swung out at 6:00 a.m. and marched to Farmville, arriving that afternoon beneath clear skies and warm sun.

"The trains were there," his men received rations, and soon the 3rd Brigade settled into a routine bivouac. "All were at rest, mind and body," Chamberlain said. He was listening to the 1st Brigade's "fine German Band" when a "mud-splashed, grave-faced, keen-eyed" courier 'rode up in front of the sentinel and the colors" and dismounted.

"Something in the manner and look of this messenger took my attention," Chamberlain said. Drawing the courier away from the assembled brigade staff, he read the "yellow tissue-paper telegram" carried by the cavalryman.

Sent from Washington, D.C., the telegram blared, "The President died this morning. Wilkes Booth the assassin. Secretary Seward dangerously wounded. The rest of the Cabinet, General Grant, and other high officers of the Government included in the plot of destruction."

Joshua Chamberlain learned about the assassination of President Abraham Lincoln while the 3rd Brigade camped at Farmville, Virginia, on Easter Sunday. (loc)

Dismissing the German band, Chamberlain immediately ordered "a double guard" flung around "the whole camp" and everyone rounded up into their regimental camps. "No one to leave," he said, and "tell the gentlemen I would like to see them here."

Brigade and regiment commanders gathered. Sharing "this appalling news," Chamberlain enjoined them not to tell "our men. They could be trusted well to bear any blow but this." Abraham Lincoln had often "come out to see" his soldiers, and "their love for the President . . . [was] something marvelous." Now "that honest, homely face" was gone from "the cowardly, brutal blow."

The division had camped on a hill overlooking Farmville, "a city, one of the nerve-centers of the rebellion," Chamberlain realized. As for his weary veterans, "it might take but little to rouse them to . . . blind revenge." Would they sack the town and attack its inhabitants?

His men must learn the news. Leaving Brig. Gen. Edwin M. Gregory "with instructions" at divisional headquarters, Chamberlain mounted and rode toward V Corps' headquarters. Then "I saw a figure often welcome to many eyes,—Charles Griffin riding up,—our corps commander now." Locating Maj. Gen. Romeyn Ayres, the generals met with Maj. Gen. George G. Meade to talk about the national disaster.

In the camps, soldiers wondered if surrendered Confederate soldiers had murdered Lincoln. Gerrish admitted that if the assassination had occurred before the April 12 paroles, "there would have been a conflict of the most deadly character." Finally told the assassin was John Wilkes Booth, an actor, "we . . . were grateful" he was not a Confederate soldier, Gerrish said.

Leaving Farmville inviolate, the disciplined Yankees marched at Monday's sunrise, blundered south toward Danville, bivouacked, and tramped to Burkeville on Tuesday, April 18. Orders held V Corps there on Wednesday while Washingtonians attended Lincoln's funeral.

"Then we thought, why not for us a funeral?" Chamberlain said. Draping black crepe on flags, "our sword hilts," and even "headquarters tents," soldiers twisted crepe into arm bands. "The minute-guns" started a "solemn boom" at noon, and the soldiers of the 1st Division stacked arms inside a hollow square also bedecked in black.

The solitary Rodman gun still mounted on Drewry's Bluff in Richmond National Battlefield Park hints at the wartime firepower available at Confederate-held Fort Darling. (bfs)

The senior chaplain, Ireland-born Father Costney Louis Egan, passionately recalled Lincoln and the shared bond between him and his warriors. The vengeful sermon stirred the men toward retaliation; "I saw them grasp as for their stacked muskets, instinctively," Chamberlain realized before grabbing Egan's arm and saying, "Turn this excitement to some good."

Then Egan blazed, "Better, thousandfold, forever better, Lincoln dead, than [Jeff] Davis living." A second Chamberlain admonishment cooled the fiery priest, and the general admitted, "Who that heard those burning woods can ever forget them?"

The 1st Division resumed its tramp on April 20, reached Wilson's Station on the Southside Railroad on April 22, and took on guard-and-provost duty from there 17 miles east to Sutherland's Station. The 2nd and 3rd divisions assumed similar responsibilities west toward Burkeville.

With frequent patrolling and, "in cases of personal violence or outrage," occasional summary trials and executions of captured criminals, the 1st Division suppressed lawless elements roaming within its jurisdiction. Chamberlain's command fed hungry civilians, reopened "mills, shops, and stores," and administered "military law" to civilians and soldiers (North and South) alike.

The shells of burned buildings line Carey Street in Richmond in April 1865. (loc)

The War Department released V Corps on Tuesday, May 2. Through Petersburg the three divisions tramped the next day, the men cheering and waving their "poor old caps" as Maj. Gen. Gouverneur K. Warren, now assigned duty in the Cockade City, watched with his staff from a hotel balcony.

Camping a few miles beyond the Appomattox River that night, the corps "marched briskly" on "the Richmond turnpike," with Chamberlain and others exploring Fort Darling at Drewry's Bluff during a mid-day break. Plagued by rain, the Yankees bivouacked at Manchester and with II Corps "crossed the James [River] on the upper pontoon bridge" and entered Richmond on May 5, Chamberlain said.

He thought the Confederate capital "a city of strange contrasts," ranging from "the charred ruins" of early April to fine houses and a George Washington statue. Then the V Corps pushed north via forced, mile-consuming marches. The divisions rotated column position daily. Some 1st Division officers diverted off the route "to visit the storied Marye's

Heights" at Fredericksburg on May 9; everyone crossed the Rappahannock the next day.

Ever Washington-ward tramped the weary soldiers on "roads rough and ragged; the hills steep and . . . the valleys swamps; the track a trap of mire," Chamberlain said.

When "a careless" teamster fired a musket and the ball struck and mortally wounded Lt. George H. Wood of the 20th Maine, "some call [it an] accident," Chamberlain rumbled. "I did not treat it as such."

Northward beneath a hellacious thunderstorm tramped the V Corps. Men debated why the government mandated a long march on May 11, and Chamberlain figured presciently "we were . . . only going to be mustered out" soon, to reduce Washington's war-related costs. Stepping off at 9:00 a.m., Tuesday, May 12, V Corps trundled onto the Columbia Pike and pressed on "to . . . permanent camp on Arlington Heights," the brigadier noted.

"We passed by Fairfax Court House, and knew that we were rapidly nearing . . . Washington," and "our marches were to be over," said the weary Theodore Gerrish. "We unconsciously increased our speed," then climbed "another steep ascent—it was Arlington heights—and we knew that from its top we could see . . . Washington."

Passing by Fairfax Court House on May 12, weary V Corps infantrymen knew they were approaching Washington, D.C., and the end of their military service. (loc)

Cresting Arlington, the 1st Division lads gazed across a fog bank lying over Washington. Then the sun burned away the low clouds, and sunlight illuminated the capital. "Soon we saw it in all its beauty," said the awe-struck Gerrish.

The V Corps camped that night on Arlington Heights, "and for the last time we pitched our shelter tents on the soil of Virginia," he said.

The End of It All

CHAPTER THIRTEEN

MAY 23, 1865 – JANUARY 16, 1866

Anxious to cut military spending, the Johnson administration scheduled a "Grand Review" to honor its warriors in late May 1865—and hustled them home as soon as possible afterwards.

Commanding the 1st Division, Brig. Gen. Joshua L. Chamberlain led the V Corps' infantry and artillery in the first parade, scheduled for Monday, May 23. The day dawned "clear, bright," and V Corps stirred early. The parade would follow Pennsylvania Avenue past "the State Department building" and a large reviewing stand erected outside the White House. The "regiments, brigades, and divisions" formed "by companies closed in mass," each company's front line 20 soldiers wide, Chamberlain noticed.

Kicking off the Grand Review, Maj. Gen. George G. Meade and "his principal staff" spurred their horses at 9:00 a.m. The Cavalry Corps followed, then the Signal Corps—perhaps even "those that beckoned us to the salvation of Round Top"—and the engineers with their pontoon boats, said Chamberlain.

"The signal sounds," and Maj. Gen. Charles Griffin sprang "lightly . . . to the saddle. Around him group the [V Corps] staff," Chamberlain noted.

"My bugle calls. Our horses know it," he said. His staff spread behind him; a young soldier bore the 1st Division's flag, "the red cross on its battle-stained white." Its ranks swollen by soldiers returned from temporary duty, the division stepped out "up the avenue" 10,000 men strong.

Disputing Maine's 1879 election results, armed dissidents occupied the State House until Joshua Chamberlain, the state's militia commander, evicted them nonviolently in January 1880. (bfs)

Cheering admirers lined the route, jammed "windows, balconies, house-tops, high and far," Chamberlain said. The V Corps reached the State Department; a bugle blew, and the soldiers shifted from "'route step' and right shoulder arms" to "the cadenced step and the shoulder arms," the stipulated position for a review.

The 1st Division finally approached the reviewing stand, and President Andrew Johnson stood for the V Corps. Wheeling Charlemagne toward the dignitaries, Chamberlain saluted. Invited with certain other generals to join Johnson's entourage, he soon dismounted and climbed into the reviewing stand to "join those at the front."

Emotion tugging at heart and memory, he watched V Corps pass into history. "These were my men," he said as the 1st Division marched by, "and those who followed were familiar and dear."

Gradually the marching soldiers all passed the White House and returned to their Virginia camps. "The day is over," said Chamberlain.

As summer approached, the War Department mustered

Many Maine soldiers, including Joshua Chamberlain, remembered crossing the Long Bridge to participate in the Grand Review in late May 1865. (loc)

out most volunteer units. Some, including a few Maine regiments, went south on occupation duty. Others joined the Provisional Corps, created on Wednesday, June 28 by consolidating "each . . . existing corps" into a division: the 1st, from VI Corps; the 2nd, from II Corps; and the 3rd, drawn from V Corps and commanded by Maj. Gen. Romeyn B. Ayres.

Each division comprised three brigades, and Chamberlain got the 3rd Brigade of Ayres's division on June 28. The corps' commander, Maj. Gen. Horatio G. Wright, soon marched his temporary outfit "to some healthy location on the Baltimore and Ohio Railroad, west of the Monocacy" River to camp near "facilities for supplying the command."

The move also placed three combat divisions where the B & O could swiftly transport them west, and the rumors abounded. Sent to the Rio Grande

Dust obscures the distant Capitol as Union cavalry ride along Pennsylvania Avenue during the Grand Review. (loc)

earlier that spring in case Emperor Maximilian's French troops invaded Texas, Maj. Gen. Philip Sheridan had missed the Grand Review. Perhaps the three-division Provisional Corps would ship south if Sheridan needed help?

And June 28 saw Meade announce via General Order No. 35 that "this army [of the Potomac], as an organization, ceases to exist."

"'Ceases to exist!'" Chamberlain exclaimed. "Are you sure of that?"

Plagued by his Petersburg wound, he stayed in Washington until later in July. Paperwork flew about a final promotion. On April 13, Charles Griffin had recommended him for promotion to brevet major general "for conspicuous gallant and meritorious service" during the Appomattox campaign.

A June 15 letter from Secretary of War Edwin Stanton informed Chamberlain that President Johnson had appointed him brevet major general, effective April 9. The brigadier spoke and signed the oath of office at his Arlington, Virginia camp on July 1. Eighteen days later, Griffin asked the army's adjutant general, Lorenzo Thomas, to back date Chamberlain's promotion "to March 29th 1865," the "date that he handled his brigade with special ability." The request generated a second brevet notice received by Chamberlain on July 21.

Arriving home late that month, he relaxed with Fanny and their three children. Only seven months old, Gertrude Loraine suddenly fell sick, and for the third time Joshua and Fanny lost a child when their daughter died on August 15. The heartbroken parents

Army units passing the presidential reviewing stand outside the White House extended President Andrew Johnson the proper recognition. (loc)

Edwin Stanton was nominated to the Supreme Court by President Ulysses S. Grant in 1869. Stanton died days after the U.S. Senate confirmed the nomination. (na)

grieved privately after burying Gertrude in the family's small Pine Grove Cemetery lot.

To compound the brigadier's emotional stress, the War Department could not leave Chamberlain alone. Issued on August 24, General Order No. 135 identified many major and brigadier generals discharged from the army. Still suffering from his Petersburg wound, Chamberlain read his name on the list. He had caught Confederate lead, led his men to victories from Little Round Top to Five Forks, and now the army had kicked him out?

He discussed the issue during an autumn meeting with Governor Samuel Cony. Without asking the battered brigadier, the governor contacted Maine Senator Lot Morrill, who with Senator William P. Fessenden and four Maine congressional representatives wrote Andrew Johnson on December 20. Their two-line paragraph requested that Chamberlain "be restored to the service."

His disabling war wounds prevented him "from prosecuting his duties in civil life," and "his [August 1865] muster out . . . was contrary to the rule then established," wrote another signatory. "I would now respectfully recommend" Chamberlain return to military service and that his muster-out date change to January 15, 1866.

"I understand Gen. Chamberlain has yet to undergo a severe surgical operation before he can possibly recover from the wound received in 1864," the signatory, Lt. Gen. Ulysses S. Grant, added his two-paragraph endorsement on Wednesday, January 16, 1866. Johnson approved the request the same day.

Some three and a half years after donning his country's uniform, Joshua L. Chamberlain set it aside and passed into Maine lore. Home from the war, he returned to Bowdoin College as a professor and as its temporary president. Only months passed, however, before his attention shifted beyond an academician's staid life.

Realizing that Chamberlain enjoyed a statewide name recognition almost equal to Grant, Sheridan, or Sherman, the Republican party nominated him for governor in June 1866 to replace Cony, intent on stepping down. Capturing a record 62.4-percent vote in the September election, he took office in January 1867 and moved to Augusta for his official duties.

Joshua Chamberlain was the first four-term governor of Maine. (msa)

Fanny opted for Brunswick, and the Chamberlains often lived apart as Joshua served four full terms, completing his last term in early January 1871. Although he desired an appointment to the U.S. Senate (the legislatures selected senators then), he lacked a politician's deal-making skills and, particularly due to opposition by Republican powerhouse James G. Blaine, never became a senator.

Bowdoin's trustees and overseers hired Chamberlain as the college's president in 1871. Financially secure, he and Fanny moved and enlarged their house and in 1879 purchased five aces at Simpsons Point on Brunswick's southern shore. There, the Chamberlains remodeled

the existing building into a summer home called "Domhegan" and kept his yacht, a twin-masted schooner he named Pinafore, at the wharf. He resumed aboard the schooner the sailing joys from his Brewer youth.

Joshua and Fanny Chamberlain paid $2,100 for this house on Potter Street in Brunswick, Maine in 1859. (phcc)

He brought the battle-scarred Charlemagne to live out its life at Domhegan. The general buried his faithful horse there at a site not accurately identified. The property later transferred to new owners; a fire tore through the rambling summer home on May 9,

Moved to a Maine Street lot in 1871, the Chamberlain house was raised so a new first floor could be added. (bfs)

The oldest of the Chamberlains' five children, Grace Dupee "Daisy" Chamberlain was born on October 16, 1856. (phcc)

Harold Wyllys Chamberlain was born in Brunswick, Maine on October 10, 1858. (phcc)

1940, and except for the wharf's foundation, little evidence connects the land to Chamberlain today.

As a U.S. commissioner of education, he took Fanny, Grace, and Wyllys (Harold's preferred name) to Europe in 1878. Then, the divisive 1879 Maine gubernatorial election left no clear winner, ignited partisan passions, and threatened civil warfare.

Armed civilians (including many veterans) took over the State House, so outgoing Governor Alonzo Garcelon brought Maj. Gen. Chamberlain, commanding the state militia, to Augusta in January 1880 to deal with the situation. Kicking out the firearm-toting mob, he called in Augusta policemen to keep order and held the State House until the Maine Supreme Judicial Court declared Daniel Davis the new governor.

Leaving Bowdoin in 1883, Chamberlain pursued various endeavors, including land speculation and railroad development in Florida and finance in New York City. Plagued by his Petersburg wound and its affiliated medical complications and pain, he paid for additional surgeries, none wholly successful. His malaria recurred, too.

Fanny suffered many years from failing eyesight and went blind. She often relied on her husband (when present) and Wyllys and Grace (married in 1881 to Boston attorney Horace Allen) for necessary care. The Allens provided Joshua and Fanny with three granddaughters on whom the Chamberlains doted. After graduating from Bowdoin, Wyllys became a lawyer and later an inventor.

In 1900, President William McKinley named Joshua Chamberlain surveyor of the port for Portland, a position offering a steady income. His beloved Fanny died on October 18, 1905; although often not home since joining the army 43 years earlier, Joshua had loved her deeply.

Represented by the memories and the Petersburg wound, the Civil War never left Chamberlain and ultimately killed him. He remained active in the Grand Army of the Republic and other veteran organizations; a skilled orator, Chamberlain often appeared at regimental reunions and participated in the day-long dedication of Maine monuments at Gettysburg on October 3, 1889.

Appointed the Bowdoin College president in 1871, Joshua Chamberlain had an office in Massachusetts Hall. (sg)

Weakened by wound-related infection and pneumonia, the 85-year-old Joshua Chamberlain died in Portland on February 24, 1914. After a state funeral held inside Merrill Auditorium at Portland City Hall, the casket traveled by train to Brunswick. Mourners lined the streets to watch as Chamberlain was transported to the family lot in Pine Grove Cemetery, next to the wrought-iron fence separating the cemetery from an adjacent stand of white pines.

Maine's warrior professor had come home for good.

His health failing, the elderly Joshua Chamberlain died inside the two-story, wood-framed house at 499 Ocean Avenue in Portland on February 14, 1914. (bfs)

Joshua L. Chamberlain Sites to Visit in Maine

APPENDIX A

Although Joshua L. Chamberlain was affiliated primarily with Brewer and Brunswick, other sites in Maine are also associated with him. Fans can check out all these Chamberlain-related sites during a driving tour of the Pine Tree State.

Portland

United States Custom House

312 Fore Street.

Designed by architect Alfred B. Mullett, the Custom House opened in 1868. Joshua L. Chamberlain had an office here after President William McKinley named him the surveyor of the port for Portland in 1900.

499 Ocean Avenue (Route 9).

Chamberlain died in this modest, white-painted frame house at age 85 on February 24, 1914. The house is privately owned.

Gorham

Civil War monument

College Street.

The monument is located between the street and the former Gorham Town House. Joshua Chamberlain spoke when the monument was dedicated on October 18, 1866.

Chamberlain Freedom Park in Brewer incorporates Maine's Underground Railroad Monument, featuring an escaped slave emerging from a tunnel. (bfs)

As surveyor of the port, Joshua Chamberlain had an office at the United States Custom House in Portland. (bfs)

Freeport

Civil War monument
Town House Square

The monument is located on South Street a short distance from L.L. Bean. Chamberlain spoke during the monument's dedication on May 26, 1906.

The Civil War monument in Freeport is a few blocks from L. L. Bean. (bfs)

Brunswick

Joshua L. Chamberlain Museum

226 Maine Street.

Acquired by the Pejepscot History Center in 1983, the house was erected at 4 Potter Street between 1824 and 1830. Renting the house in 1856, Chamberlain paid $2,100 for it in 1859. He and Fanny had the house, then a two-story cape, moved nearer Maine Street in 1867 and extensively enlarged the house in 1871. Restored to its Chamberlain-era appearance, the house contains a large collection of Chamberlain family artifacts, including some original furnishings.

The museum is open for tours from Tuesday through Sunday, Memorial Day weekend to Columbus Day weekend and then from Friday through Sunday until Veterans Day. Call 207-729-6606 or log onto www.pejepscothistorical.org.

Joshua Chamberlain statue

Located across Maine Street from the Chamberlain Museum. This 8-foot bronze sculpture was created by Joseph Query and was dedicated in 2003.

First Parish Church

9 Cleaveland Street.

A Greek Revival-style building constructed in 1845, this church was where Joshua and Fanny Chamberlain were married by her father, Reverend George E. Adams, in December 1855.

The Pejepscot History Center Museum and Research Center

159 Park Row.

The center has a comprehensive Chamberlain-related research collection, including printed material and photographs. The research center is open Tuesday through Sunday from Memorial Day weekend to Columbus Day weekend and Wednesday through Friday otherwise. Call 207-729-6606 or log onto www.pejepscothistorical.org.

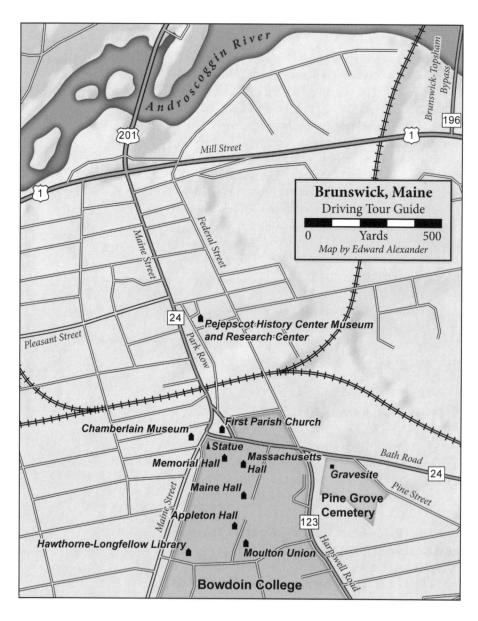

BRUNSWICK, MAINE DRIVING TOUR GUIDE—The multiple sites associated with Joshua Chamberlain in Brunswick are within an easy walk of each other.

Pine Grove Cemetery on the Bath Road (Route 24). Enter the first gate and walk to the Chamberlain family lot on the right, just four lots inside the cemetery.

Several **Bowdoin College** buildings are affiliated with Chamberlain.
The campus is located at the intersection of Maine Street and Bath Road.

Appleton Hall
Chamberlain lived in room 19 while a freshman.

Maine Hall
His next three years at Bowdoin, Chamberlain lived in room 32 and room 21.

Massachusetts Hall
During his Bowdoin College presidency, Chamberlain used an office on the first floor.

Memorial Hall
During his Bowdoin presidency, Chamberlain utilized this building for military drill, which he instituted and which the students did not receive well.

During his presidency, Joshua Chamberlain instituted military drill for all Bowdoin College students. The drill took place in Memorial Hall. (sg)

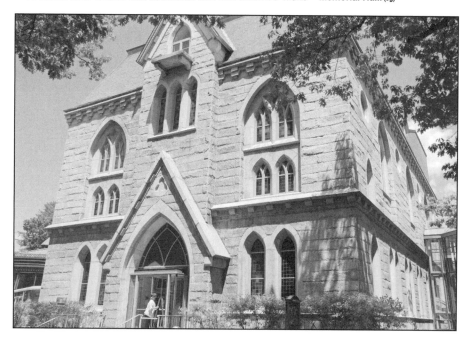

Joshua and Fanny Chamberlain and several family members are buried in the Pine Grove Cemetery near Bowdoin College. (bfs)

Moulton Union

A Dale Gallon painting depicting Chamberlain at Little Round Top hangs on the first floor. A second-floor meeting room displays photographs covering Chamberlain's years at Bowdoin as a student, a professor, and its president.

Hawthorne-Longfellow Library

The George J. Mitchell Department of Special Collections & Archives contains extensive Chamberlain-related documents, some photographs, his 1893 Medal of Honor, and the Tiffany bracelet that Chamberlain gave Fanny.

Augusta

Maine State House

Located on State Street overlooking Capitol Park. Designed by architect Charles Bullfinch, the State House opened officially with a legislative session in January 1832. The executive office of Governor Joshua L. Chamberlain was located here during his four terms in 1867, 1868, 1869, and 1870.

The State House gained its current appearance with an extensive modernization and expansion in the early twentieth century.

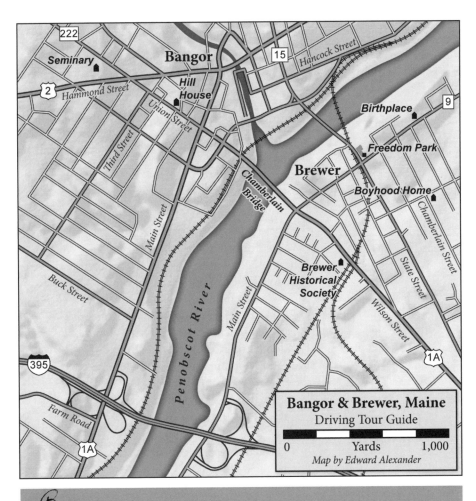

Bangor & Brewer, Maine
Driving Tour Guide

0   Yards   1,000

Map by Edward Alexander

Brewer

Chamberlain Freedom Park

Intersection of North Main Street (Route 9) and State Street, with parking available at the adjacent convenience store or in a small lot at the base of State Street hill.

After the Maine Department of Transportation tore down the 1811 Holyoke House to widen the intersection in the 1990s, local historians spearheaded creating this park on the slope above State Street.

Designed to resemble Little Round Top, **Chamberlain Freedom Park** incorporates a Chamberlain statue, a down-sized version of the 20th Maine monument at Little Round Top, information placards, and a worm fence similar to those found at Gettysburg.

BANGOR & BREWER, MAINE DRIVING TOUR GUIDE—Among the several sites in Bangor and Brewer associated with Joshua L. Chamberlain are his birthplace and his childhood home.

A Joshua Chamberlain statue stands beyond the replica 20th Maine monument at Chamberlain Freedom Park in Brewer. (bfs)

According to long-held local lore, a tunnel connected the Brewer waterfront with the Holyoke House cellar. Escaping slaves spirited up the Penobscot River could scuttle through the tunnel and find shelter in the house before fleeing to New Brunswick.

To commemorate this tale, the Chamberlain Freedom Park also incorporates Maine's Underground Railroad Monument, a bronze statue of an escaped slave emerging from a tunnel.

Chamberlain Birthplace

350 North Main Street.

Located between the road and the Penobscot River, this house was built by Chamberlain's father, Joshua, and here Lawrence Joshua Chamberlain was born on September 8, 1828. A high stockade fence now blocks street-level views of the house, privately owned and not open to the public.

Joshua L. Chamberlain grew up in the house that his father built at 80 Chamberlain Street in Brewer. (bfs)

Chamberlain Boyhood Home

80 Chamberlain Street, at the intersection with Washington Street.

Joshua Chamberlain built this house circa 1836, and his children grew up there. Although privately owned and not open to the public, the house can be viewed from the street.

Clewley Museum

199 Wilson Street.
Containing some Chamberlain-related photographs, the museum is operated by the Brewer Historical Society.

Thomas A. Hill House

159 Union Street.
Now home to the Bangor Historical Society, this Greek Revival-style brick mansion was built in 1836 for Bangor attorney Thomas A. Hill.

The mansion houses an extensive historical collection, including the sword and scabbard worn by Col. Joshua L. Chamberlain at Little Round Top. The dent where a Confederate bullet smacked the scabbard, inflicting a bruise to Chamberlain's left thigh, is clearly visible.

The Hill House is open for tours. Contact 207-942-1900 or log onto www.bangorhistoricalsociety.org.

The Thomas A. Hill House in Bangor was a GAR post for many years after the Civil War. (bhs)

Bangor Theological Seminary

Between Hammond and Union streets.
Although it closed in June 2013, the seminary lives on in several buildings extant when Joshua L. Chamberlain studied there in the 1850s.

Opened in November 1954, the two-lane **Joshua L. Chamberlain Bridge** connects Union Street in Bangor with Wilson Street in Brewer. The bridge is the middle of the three highway bridges between the two cities.

"Do not scorn what is brought in love": The Complicated Relationship of Joshua and Fanny

APPENDIX B

BY ASHLEY TOWLE, PH.D.

While most biographies of Joshua Chamberlain focus on his military successes and postwar achievements, less attention has been paid to his personal life and, in particular, his relationship with his wife, Fanny.

Historians who have examined the Chamberlains' marriage offer conflicting characterizations of their relationship. Some contend that Fanny had a selfish and willful nature and that her frivolous spending habits led to a deep rift in their union. Others concede that while their union was sometimes turbulent, the Chamberlains ultimately remained together for more than 50 years and served as each other's primary source of support.

What emerges from both the archives and historians' analysis is a complicated relationship between two independent people. Joshua's years at war and as Maine governor strained their relationship but did not break it. And in their older years, when both suffered from failing health, they found comfort in one another.

Fanny and Joshua's initial courtship reveals her strong independent streak and Joshua's insecurity and dependence on her for affection and validation. The couple met in 1850 in the First Parish Church, where Fanny's adopted father, Reverend George Adams, preached and Joshua directed the church choir.

As the relationship developed, Fanny had reservations about marrying Joshua. She conveyed these concerns to a friend who provided some telling advice. "You say you love him--yet do not feel that sort of love for him of which you dreamed so wildly . . . I guess that hints from you suggest that he is of a rather jealous, sanguine and ardent temperament, that makes large demands and might be hard to please or satisfy. If you cannot satisfy him now and inspire powerful confidence, you never will."

Fanny accepted Joshua's proposal in May 1852.

Within their cherished home in Brunswick, Fanny and Joshua Chamberlain raised their children and perhaps sometimes found shelter from the issues threatening their marital relationship. (bfs)

The couple postponed their marriage until Joshua finished his studies at the Bangor Theological Seminary. Meanwhile, Fanny indulged her artistic pursuits and studied music in New York City before teaching music at a female academy in Milledgeville, Georgia. Although dismayed at their separation, Joshua supported her endeavors, noting, "I see now the wisdom as well as the nobleness & independence of your present resolution & undertaking. I honor & respect you even more than I ever have."

After a long year and a half, Fanny encouraged Joshua to re-think his ministerial career in favor of becoming a teacher so that they could be married sooner. She believed herself unfit by "mind, character and temperament" to be a minister's wife, acknowledging that she had a taste for fine clothing and luxurious goods.

Joshua persevered, graduating from the seminary in August 1855. He refused to marry Fanny until he secured a well-paying job as a Bowdoin College teacher. Finally, on December 7, 1855, Fanny and Joshua were wed.

The early years of their marriage were filled with joy and sadness. The couple had two children, Grace and Harold Wyllys, born in 1856 and 1858, but also suffered the deaths of another son and daughter in 1857 and 1859. Despite these losses, the Chamberlains settled into life together, building their family and home in Brunswick.

The Civil War upended this domestic peace. It is unclear how Fanny responded when Joshua decided to join the army in 1862. What their wartime letters make clear, however, is that she supported him as much as possible while he wrote of the bloodshed he witnessed.

These war-torn years tested the Chamberlains' marriage. Fanny wrote Joshua often, asking for assistance when it came to home maintenance and the upkeep of his beloved garden. They wrote to one another as frequently as possible, but their letters reveal the frustration they felt at being apart. Responding to a letter in which Fanny voiced her anxieties and loneliness, Joshua wrote, "I want you to be cheerful & occupy your mind with pleasant things, so as not to have time to grow melancholy. You mustn't think of me much."

Letters were often lost and never received, adding to Fanny's anxiety about the well-being of her husband. When she did receive his letters, Joshua confided in her about his military successes and his horror at the carnage he witnessed at Antietam, Fredericksburg, and elsewhere.

Fanny's fears of losing her husband nearly came true with his wounding at Petersburg in June 1864. Believing he was dying, Joshua scribbled a note to his "darling wife" assuring her that she had been "precious" to him. "To know & love you makes life & death beautiful," he wrote.

Fanny rushed to his side in Annapolis, Maryland and helplessly watched as he writhed in pain. At the time, she was also pregnant and likely worried that her children would be fatherless.

Bowdoin College named Joshua Chamberlain its president in 1871, a few years after his marriage faced a severe challenge. (bcl)

Joshua made a miraculous recovery and returned to Brunswick to convalesce. Archival sources are silent on how Fanny reacted when Joshua departed for battle, but one can imagine her anxiety as she neared the end of her pregnancy and wondered if her children's father would ever return home.

While Joshua survived the war's end, postwar life brought its own challenges, adjustments, and continued separations. In August 1865, Fanny and Joshua's seven-month-old child, Gertrude Loraine, died after falling ill.

While grieving her loss, the Chamberlains also adapted again to life with one another. Fanny knew that Joshua would not be the same after the war—his wartime letters had intimated as much. Physically, he never fully recovered from his wound, and his wartime experiences impelled him to a public-service career that kept him away from home.

Fanny resumed her independent travels to New York and Boston to visit friends and family. When Joshua was elected governor in 1866, she remained in Brunswick while he attended to his duties in Augusta; occasionally, she joined him for events there.

Joshua's years at war and as governor strained their marriage. Tellingly, letters between the Chamberlains are scarce during his years as governor. Existing letters reveal a marriage so fractured that by 1868, Fanny seriously contemplated a divorce.

Fanny Chamberlain anchored her husband's home life through her love, patience, and endurance. (phcc)

In a scathing letter, Joshua harangued her for confiding to a friend that he had abused her "beyond endurance" by pulling her hair and "striking, beating & otherwise personally maltreating" her. Joshua demanded that Fanny stop discussing their personal lives and end whatever divorce proceedings she had begun.

To protect his political career and the family's reputation, he proposed a separation. "You never take my advice," he lamented. "But if you do not <u>stop this</u> at once it will end in <u>hell</u>. I am sorry to say this to you, when I have so entirely confided in you. . ."

Historians have made much of this letter. It is noteworthy that Joshua never denies abusing her or insists that she stop spreading lies about their marriage. As Diane Monroe Smith pointed out, Maine was a no-fault state for divorce, so Fanny needed no justification to file for divorce.

Joshua's traumatic wartime experiences and his unsuccessful struggle to find relief from his festering wound possibly made readjusting to civilian life difficult for him, and he took his frustrations out on Fanny. While this is speculation, the letter conclusively reveals a frayed relationship in which both parties required space.

Ultimately Fanny heeded his warning and agreed to a separation. Evidence suggests that they lived apart for over a year. In fall 1869, Joshua complained to his daughter Grace that Fanny refused to answer his letters, noting, "I would write to Mamma instead of you if the little scamp would answer me."

When in Brunswick, Joshua stayed with a neighbor while Fanny remained at their home. By late 1870, it appears that somehow the Chamberlains began to reconcile and rebuild their life together.

This reconciliation likely was made easier by the frequent separations that still characterized their marriage. While serving as Bowdoin College president, Joshua pursued business ventures in Florida and New York City that meant more time away from home.

While Joshua continued to travel for business and for war-related speaking engagements, Fanny's world shrank. She lost her independence as her eyesight worsened due to a childhood condition. Eventually, she became blind and refused to leave Brunswick, making exceptions only to visit her daughter and grandchildren in Boston.

One can imagine how difficult this must have been for Fanny, considering the artistic, independent life she once had. Joshua supported her as much as possible, but it proved difficult to watch her withdraw inward. He pleaded with Fanny to accept the love and care of others. "You need love--most of anything . . . do not scorn what is brought in love. It makes you so unhappy--that is the worst of it all, & that makes me so more & more as I see your need."

Fanny died on October 18, 1905. Her funeral was held in the First Parish Church, and she was buried in the family plot in Pine Grove Cemetery in Brunswick.

After her death, Joshua left much of their Brunswick home untouched; Fanny's decor and style could still be seen throughout the home. He traveled to Brunswick less often, preferring instead to spend his time in Portland or with his grandchildren in Boston.

When Joshua died on February 24, 1914, he was laid to rest next to Fanny.

Joshua and Fanny's complicated relationship spanned more than 50 years. Through an examination of their marriage, the Chamberlains become human, rather than mythical figures.

Behind Joshua's soaring rhetoric was a man who had fears, insecurities, and weaknesses. His relationship with Fanny exposes these shortcomings as Fanny's headstrong and independent nature continually vexed him. But in his darkest moments in war and as a college president, Fanny was the one to whom Joshua turned for comfort.

For her part, Fanny also found both a source of support and frustration in their half-century union. In their old age the Chamberlains relied on one another again, just as during the war. As they suffered from poor health, their family helped them to weather the uncertainties of old age and served as a testament to the bond they had forged together, a bond often strained, but never broken.

ASHLEY TOWLE *is a Lecturer in the History Department at the University of Southern Maine. Her research and teaching interests include 19th Century United States history, the history of the American South, the history of race in the United States, and the history of gender and sexuality.*

Why Chamberlain?

APPENDIX C

BY RYAN QUINT

There is no doubt that Joshua Lawrence Chamberlain lived an extraordinary life, from his childhood in Brewer to graduating and subsequently teaching at Bowdoin College, the horrors of the Civil War, then to a four-term governorship of Maine and the presidency of his alma mater. He is certainly one of the Pine Tree State's most heralded and famed residents.

And yet it seems sometimes all those events in a very storied life are characterized in a flash, and the focus on Chamberlain, time and time again, comes to rest on a few hours' actions in the afternoon of July 2, 1863. At the head of the 20th Maine, Chamberlain gained immortality.

At face value, there is nothing especially distinguishing about the 20th Maine prior to the battle of Gettysburg. As they marched north, the Mainers numbered 386 rank and file, slightly larger than the average regiment in the Army of the Potomac, but except for that, they were like tens of thousands of other Federal soldiers going into battle.

Their fighting on July 2, while heroic and gallant, was likewise similar to so many other units that battled across the fields of Adams County, Pennsylvania. Why then, when considering the 20th Maine, do tens of thousands of visitors a year flock to their position on Little Round Top? And more pointedly, why do those same visitors discuss the regiment's colonel more than probably any other field-grade officer on either side of the battle?

The names of William Colvill or David Ireland, whose actions on July 2 are equally worthy of praise, have receded from memory. But Joshua Lawrence Chamberlain? He is a different case entirely, with poems and paintings prominently featuring him to this day.

The question remains: why?

The reason why Chamberlain has remained such a fixture in Civil War memory begins with himself. Living until 1914, Chamberlain never hesitated to tell his story and raise his status.

Maine understandably preserves the memory of Joshua L. Chamberlain, his wartime features captured in this Brunswick statue. But why does he have such a strong presence in American lore? (bfs)

Historians cannot hold that against him—he was far from the only person to do so—but it sometimes rubbed his subordinates the wrong way. Ellis Spear, his second-in-command at Gettysburg, complained over 50 years later that Chamberlain "was absolutely unable to tell the truth and was of inordinate vanity."

Nonetheless, the articles Chamberlain wrote made him a well-known figure of his time. His status as a brevet major general, a rank he obtained at the end of the war, as well as a respected politician, certainly did not hurt either.

But simply because Chamberlain wrote much about himself is not the whole story. After his death, even Chamberlain's star faded from view. While still mentioned in books about Gettysburg, Chamberlain was not elevated to hero status until the second half of the 20th century.

Three famed projects, created back to back to back, all highlighted Joshua Chamberlain and are the collective reason why he became, and remains, the most famous colonel at Gettysburg.

Michael Shaara taught creative writing and literature at

The 20th Maine monument on Little Round Top became a tourist attraction after the 1993 movie *Gettysburg*. (bfs)

Florida State University. Seeking to write a drama fit for Shakespeare, Shaara focused his attention on the battle of Gettysburg. With a cast of characters made up of the usual faces of generals like Robert E. Lee, George Pickett, John Buford, and Winfield S. Hancock, Shaara also included Chamberlain. Here was his outlier, a professor of rhetoric, not a West Point graduate.

Shaara got to writing *The Killer Angels*, which was published in 1974. A year later it earned the Pulitzer Prize for Fiction and has been read by millions ever since. Shaara's depiction of the fighting atop Little Round Top puts Chamberlain front and center. Each attack that wears down the 20th Maine and empties their cartridge boxes forces Chamberlain to act.

Finally, with no ammunition left, Shaara's version of Chamberlain makes a spur of the moment decision to swing his battered regiment down "like a door" into the Confederates.

Historians have argued until the cows came home about what actually happened on top of Little Round Top. Debate has flowed back and forth over who really deserved credit for the 20th Maine's countercharge. That debate started with Ellis Spear, who bristled as Chamberlain claimed credit and praise for the attack, and continued into the twentieth century.

Yet none of that mattered in *The Killer Angels*. It was Chamberlain, and Chamberlain alone, who orchestrated the movement that won the day. That was the version of events read by all those millions of readers, and it was that version of events that stuck. Shaara called Chamberlain "one of the most remarkable soldiers in American history."

It was a sentiment soon shared by others. Chamberlain's stock was rising.

By late life, his innumerable letters and memoirs and extensive participation in veterans' organizations and reunions made Joshua L. Chamberlain well known among his wartime peers and their descendants. (msa)

One person who read *The Killer Angels* was the 31-year-old documentarian Ken Burns, who had created a film about the Brooklyn Bridge that received the Academy Award for Best Documentary, and another film about the Statue of Liberty that garnered another Academy nomination. Burns was on the lookout for his next project.

He finished reading Shaara's work on Christmas Day 1984 and was hooked by one character in particular. As he wrote later, "What was important to me about the book was that it introduced me, for the first time, to Joshua Lawrence Chamberlain."

Burns added, "For all intents and purposes, it was the life of Chamberlain which convinced me to embark on the most difficult and satisfying experience of my life."

Burns' *The Civil War* premiered in September 1990. With nine episodes that totalled nearly 12 hours, Burns brought the war into homes of millions of Americans. By all accounts, the documentary was another smash hit for Burns, with its slow panning across thousands of photos, somber music, and an ensemble of interviewed historians and voice actors.

Fewer Chamberlain fans ascend Big Round Top to visit the 20th Maine monument erected there. (bfs)

When one considers Burns's inspiration, it is unsurprising that he decides to devote almost 10 minutes detailing the 20th Maine's fighting on Little Round Top. In a documentary concerning the entire war, where major events such as Sherman's Atlanta campaign did not even get ten minutes, here is a blow by blow account of the action.

The narrative draws heavily on an ethos-driven approach and is certainly stirring. Chamberlain, in Burns's narrative, executes "an unlikely textbook maneuver" that wins the day and even potentially saves the Union.

There are problems, historically speaking, though. Historian Thomas Desjardin wrote, "Never mind that there is no textbook or that there was no 'maneuver' in the sense Burns describes, or even that in his lifetime Chamberlain repeatedly denied ordering a charge. He is as heroically American as modern legend can be—or needs to be."

The criticism would come later, though. For now, following on the heels of Shaara's publication, Burns's documentary elevated Chamberlain once again.

The success of *The Civil War* inspired the third project. This one would see Shaara's novel put to film. Directed by Ron Maxwell, the movie, with a simpler, straightforward *Gettysburg* as its title, was released in 1993. With Jeff Daniels portraying Chamberlain, the film was a faithful adaptation of Shaara's writing, though the author did not live to see it, having died of a heart attack in 1988.

Audiences watched as Chamberlain, standing his ground on the "end of the line," fought on. They watched as he gathered his officers together to explain their swinging-door attack that by now had become so famous in the public perception of the fighting atop Little Round Top. "Bayonets!" Chamberlain screams, the music swells, and the Mainers go streaming down the hilltop.

The trifecta was complete: Chamberlain had become a household name and, more than that, a household hero. Desjardin, writing of Chamberlain's canonization, notes, "A member of the now enormous Chamberlain fan club can drink Chamberlain pale ale from a Chamberlain coffee mug propped up against a Chamberlain pillow, spying a Chamberlain wall clock or wristwatch."

But the story does not end there. Shaara, Burns, and Maxwell's *Gettysburg* pushed Chamberlain up, but what has kept him there are legions of artists. Quite simply, painters paint what sells, and from the mid-1990s to today, Chamberlain sells. As historian Gary Gallagher writes, "A subject of no importance in Civil War artworks produced in the nineteenth century, Chamberlain has become the most-painted United States military officer." More to the point, Gallagher notes, "Chamberlain boasts more than twice as many pieces as Grant and fives times the number of Sherman, Sheridan, McClellan and Meade combined."

If one takes a moment to contemplate that, the conclusion is staggering. Grant, arguably the most successful general of the entire war, *and* a president of the United States, stands in the shadows of a single regimental commander.

Of course, Chamberlain's career continued, with more fame because of his role in the surrender at Appomattox, but the overwhelming majority of artwork and depictions show him as that colonel from Maine standing among the rocks of Little Round Top.

As long as people continue to read *The Killer Angels*, re-watch *The Civil War* and *Gettysburg*, or buy artwork from their favorite artists, Chamberlain will remain above the rest. It would surely drive the likes of Ellis Spear crazy, but Chamberlain, the man himself?

He'd be just fine with it.

RYAN QUINT, a Maine native, lives in Virginia and works for the National Park Service. He is the author of Determined to Stand and Fight: The Battle of Monocacy, July 9, 1864.

Suggested Reading

The Civil War Recollections of General Ellis Spear
Abbott Spear, Andrea C. Hawkes, Marie H. McCosh,
Craig L. Symonds, and Michael H. Alpert, editors
The University of Maine Press (1997)
ISBN-0891010947

Incorporating three unpublished accounts written
by Ellis Spear, this book provides significant insight
into Spear's role within the 20th Maine. Included
are his 1863-1865 diaries, his Personal Memoranda
from 1896, and his Recollections, written circa 1904
to 1918.

"Bayonet! Forward" My Civil War Reminiscences
Joshua Lawrence Chamberlain
Stan Clark Military Books (1994)
ISBN-13:9781879664210

Joshua Chamberlain discusses the war in his own
"voice" in this time-limited biography that opens with
Fredericksburg and closes with the Grand Review. Of
particular interest is the chapter titled "Reminiscences
of Petersburg and Appomattox," written after
Chamberlain's postwar visit to both battlefields. The
appendices include some wartime correspondence,
reports, and speeches.

The Grand Old Man of Maine: Selected Letters of Joshua Lawrence Chamberlain 1865-1914
Jeremiah E. Coulka, editor
The University of North Carolina Press (2004)
ISBN-13:9780807828649

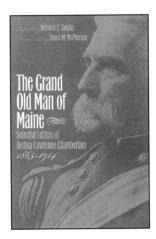

This anthology explores the postwar life of Joshua L. Chamberlain via his correspondence, which flows chronologically through five chapters to a last letter written 20 days before his death. Undated letters appear in the appendix, and editor Jeremiah Coulka liberally uses footnotes to explain the human-and-event references made in many letters.

His Proper Post: A Biography of Gen. Joshua Lawrence Chamberlain
Sis Deans
Belle Grove Publishing Company (1996)
ISBN-13:978188392076

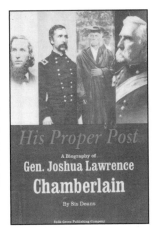

Illustrated with maps and photographs, His Proper Post offers young and new Chamberlain fans an easy-to-read biography packing a lot of information (including multiple-source footnotes) within 159 pages. This is a good introductory book for people meeting Chamberlain for the first time.

Stand Firm Ye Boys From Maine: The 20th Maine and the Gettysburg Campaign
Thomas A. Desjardin
Thomas Publications (1995)
ISBN-0-939631-89-X

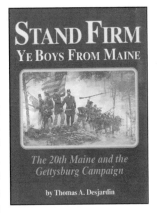

Definitely not just another Chamberlain-at-Gettysburg yarn, this first-class history concentrates on the 20th Maine's role in the overall campaign, not just at Little Round Top. Drawing upon letters and memoirs from all ranks, historian and author Tom Desjardin puts the reader in the line of battle, where gunsmoke swirls and rifles flame. Readers will particularly value the accompanying maps.

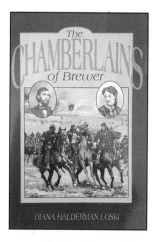

The Chamberlains of Brewer
Diana Halderman Loski
Thomas Publications (1998)
ISBN: 1-57747-038-9

Diana Loski, a Licensed Battlefield Guide in Gettysburg, explores the stories of the parents, siblings, and spouse of Joshua Chamberlain, offering an excellent family portrait and history.

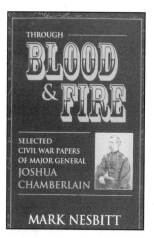

Through Blood & Fire: Selected Civil War Papers of Major General Joshua Chamberlain
Mark Nesbitt
Stackpole Books (1996)
ISBN-13: 9780811731294

The reader pleasantly discovers that despite its title, this well-written book is actually much more than a correspondence collection. In his clear prose, author Mark Nesbitt blends Chamberlain's letters and reports with his army service to explain what's happening as Joshua Chamberlain writes his way from Bowdoin College into uniform and back again.

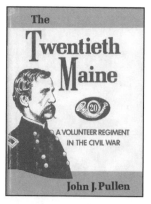

Twentieth Maine: A Volunteer Regiment in the Civil War
John J. Pullen
Morningside House Inc. (1991)
ISBN-13:9780890297551

John J. Pullen presents the history of Maine's best-known infantry regiment in a Bruce Catton storytelling style that keeps the reader glued to the pages. Well-detailed and filled with soldiers renowned and obscure, the book explains how civilians became warriors fighting capably on many battlefields.

Fanny & Joshua: The Enigmatic Lives of Frances Caroline Adams and Joshua Lawrence Chamberlain
Diane Monroe Smith
Thomas Publications (1999)
ISBN-13: 978-1611684391

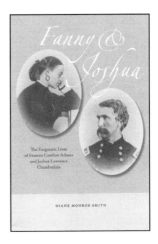

The loving, occasionally tumultuous relationship between Joshua and Frances Chamberlain comes alive in this exquisitely detailed book. Writing as if she peered directly into the Chamberlain home through history's telescope, author Diane Monroe Smith presents Chamberlain the husband and father and warrior, and Frances comes alive as a three-dimensional woman with her own interests, desires, and fears. Other Chamberlain friends and relatives appear in their respective roles, helping round out just who Fanny and Joshua were.

In the Hands of Providence: Joshua Chamberlain & The American Civil War
Alice Rains Trulock
The University of North Carolina Press (1992)
ISBN 0-8078-4980-4

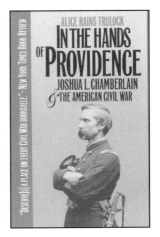

Thoroughly researched and footnoted, this exemplary biography focuses on the war as experienced by Chamberlain, from his initial enlistment with the 20th Maine to his departure from the army. Readers will savor the historic minutiae found in Trulock's extensive footnotes, often expanded to provide additional information beyond the cited source.

About the Author

After a 27-year career as a reporter and editor with the *Bangor Daily News* in Maine, Brian Swartz retired to pursue other writing interests, especially books pertaining to the Civil War and Maine history. He publishes the weekly Maine at War blog, reports for a coastal Maine newspaper, and writes for a history magazine.

A descendant of a Civil War soldier, Brian resides in Hampden, Maine, with his wife, Susan, and their cat, Miss Getty, short for "Gettysburg."